PAYROLL
Accounting

tutorial

NVQ LEVEL 2
ACCOUNTING

Michael Fardon

consultants:
Susan Dineen
Roger Petheram
McKnight Winwood & Co

OSBORNE
BOOKS

Published by Osborne Books Limited
Unit 1B Everoak Estate
Bromyard Road
Worcester
WR2 5HN
Tel 01905 748071
Email books@osborne.u-net.com
www.osbornebooks.co.uk

Printed by the Bath Press, Bath.

British Library Cataloguing in Publication Data
A catalogue record for this book is available from the British Library

ISBN 1 872962 13 0

CONTENTS

ACKNOWLEDGEMENTS

The author wishes to thank the following for their help with the reading and production of the book: Michael Gilbert, Jon Moore and Anita Sherwood. Thanks are also due to the Association of Accounting Technicians for their generous help and advice and to the Lead Body for Accounting for permission to reproduce extracts from the Standards of Competence for Accounting. The publisher is grateful to the Inland Revenue, the Department of Social Security and the Contributions Agency for the provision of Tax tables and forms, which are Crown Copyright and are reproduced here with the permission of the Controller of Her Majesty's Stationery Office.

AUTHOR AND CONSULTANTS

Michael Fardon has had extensive teaching experience on a wide range of banking, business and accountancy courses at Worcester College of Technology. He now specialises in writing business and financial texts and is General Editor at Osborne Books. He is also an educational consultant and has worked extensively in the areas of Key Skills and GNVQ development.

Particular thanks go to our consultants on this project. Roger Petheram, who has for a number of years taught payroll to students at Worcester College of Technology, has provided invaluable help in structuring the text so that it can readily be taught – expanding on difficult areas and judiciously cutting down on unnecessary detail. Osborne Books is also pleased to have involved McKnight Winwood & Co, a Worcestershire firm of Chartered Certified Accountants, whose tax manager John Elliott has provided specialist tax and payroll advice. Thanks are also due to Susan Dineen who has helped to revise and update the text to bring it line with current taxation practice for the 1999/2000 tax year.

INTRODUCTION

Osborne tutorials

Payroll Accounting Tutorial has been written to provide a study resource for students taking courses based on the NVQ Level 2 Accounting standards such as the AAT Foundation and ACCA technician level course. The text covers the NVQ 'Recording Payroll Transactions' unit. The areas of accounting for cash and credit transactions are covered by the companion Osborne texts *Cash & Credit Accounting Tutorial* and *Cash & Credit Accounting Workbook*.

Operating payroll is at the same time very complex and very straightforward. The structure of all the deductions and all the variations that occur can seem daunting, but in essence payroll is simple, once the fundamental principles are understood and have been practised. *Payroll Accounting Tutorial* provides the student with the theoretical background to the subject while at the same time including plenty of opportunity to put theory into practice. The aim has been to introduce the right amount of material at the right level, avoiding the temptation to overburden the student with unnecessary detail.

The chapters of *Payroll Accounting Tutorial* contain:

- a clear text with worked examples and case studies
- a chapter summary and key terms to help with revision
- student activities – with answers at the end of the book

The tutorial text is therefore useful for classroom use and also for distance learning students. More extended student exercises, without answers in the text, are available in the *Payroll Accounting Workbook* (see below).

Users of this text are advised, for further guidance, to obtain resources from the Inland Revenue, such as the *Employer's Quick Guide to PAYE and NICs* (which are published in the form of reference cards), the *Employer's Further Guide to PAYE and NICs*, and up-to-date tax and National Insurance tables.

Osborne workbooks

Payroll Accounting Tutorial has been written to be used alongside the *Payroll Accounting Workbook* which contains extended student activities and sample Devolved Assessments.

The answers to these tasks are included in a separate *Tutor Pack*.

If you would like a workbook, please telephone Osborne Books' Sales Office on 01905 748071 for details of ordering by credit card, or by cheque.

COVERAGE OF NVQ COMPETENCES

UNIT 3: RECORDING PAYROLL TRANSACTIONS

element 1

operate and maintain a payroll accounting system   *chapter*

❏ *gross earnings are properly authorised, correctly calculated and coded*	*2*
❏ *the current authorised payroll status of employees is accurately recorded*	*3,4,5,6*
❏ *records of gross employee earnings are correctly transferred to the payroll*	*2*
❏ *statutory and non-statutory deductions are correctly calculated and made in accordance with legal and organisational requirements*	*3,4,5,6*
❏ *a summary and analysis of the payroll is accurately transferred to the correct ledger accounts*	*9*
❏ *the organisation's policies procedures and timescales are observed*	*2,3,4,5,6,9*
❏ *confidentiality and security of information is maintained*	*1,9*
❏ *discrepancies, unusual features or queries are identified and referred to the appropriate person or resolved*	*9*
❏ *documentation is correctly filed*	*1*

element 2

make authorised payments to employees

❏ *payslip advice records are correctly prepared and reconciled with cash records*	*7*
❏ *due payments are correctly processed within specified deadlines*	*7*
❏ *payroll information is clearly explained to employees and enquiries from employees are handled courteously and confidentially*	*7*
❏ *annual tax records and other relevant documentation is made available to employees promptly*	*7*
❏ *defined procedures for dealing with unclaimed pay are strictly followed*	*7*
❏ *safety and security procedures for the handling of cash and cheques are always followed*	*7*
❏ *confidentiality and security of information is maintained*	*7*
❏ *discrepancies, unusual features or queries are identified and referred to the appropriate person or resolved*	*7*
❏ *documentation is correctly filed*	*7*

element 3

make authorised payments, claims and returns to external agencies

Note

For the 'Knowledge and Understanding' requirements of the course, please refer to the index for individual subjects.

1 INTRODUCTION TO PAYROLL

this chapter covers . . .

Before studying payroll in detail it is important to establish

- *the nature of the relationship between an organisation and a person working for it*
- *the difference between an employee and a self-employed person*
- *the nature of a contract of employment*
- *an overall view of the way a payroll system works*
- *the timescales involved in payroll*
- *the need to keep employee records confidential and secure*

Set out below are the NVQ competences covered by this chapter.

NVQ PERFORMANCE CRITERIA COVERED

unit 3: RECORDING PAYROLL TRANSACTIONS

element 1

operate and maintain a payroll accounting system

❑ *confidentiality and security of information is maintained*

❑ *data protection legislation*

KNOWLEDGE AND UNDERSTANDING – THE BUSINESS ENVIRONMENT

❑ *understanding of employment status*

KNOWLEDGE AND UNDERSTANDING – ACCOUNTING PRINCIPLES AND THEORY

❑ *internal check, control and security procedures*

KNOWLEDGE AND UNDERSTANDING – THE ORGANISATION

❑ *background understanding that the accounting systems of an organisation are affected by its organisational structure, its administrative systems and procedures and the nature of its business transactions*

WHO IS ON THE PAYROLL?

payroll

Payroll is a system set up by an individual or an organisation employing people which:

- records the personal details of the employees
- records the wages, salaries and other payments due to them
- arranges for the money to be paid
- calculates appropriate deductions to be made, eg income tax and National Insurance contributions
- arranges for the deductions to be paid to the appropriate authority, eg income tax and National Insurance contributions to the Inland Revenue

It goes without saying that a payroll system must be *accurate* and be kept *confidential*. Employees need to be paid the right amount and they need to be sure that the details of their pay is not circulated to all their colleagues.

self-employed or an employee?

If someone does work for an individual or an organisation it is essential to be clear about whether the person is *self-employed* or an *employee*. The reason is simple: an employee will go on the payroll, a self-employed person will not.

The employer will pay an employee through the payroll and deduct income tax and National Insurance contributions; on the other hand the employer will normally pay a self-employed person on receipt of an invoice. A self-employed person will have to settle up personally with the Inland Revenue for income tax and National Insurance contributions due (this is not covered by your studies at this stage).

Employers have, in most cases, to pay National Insurance contributions for employees as an additional expense out of their budget, but if they use self-employed people, eg plumbers and consultants, they do not have to pay National Insurance at all, or go to the administrative expense of putting that person on the payroll – which are considerable advantages!

Deciding whether a person is self-employed or not is not always as obvious as you might think. There is no legal definition of self-employment, so the decision is made by applying commonsense principles of looking at the activity undertaken by the person and the way it is carried out.

checklist for self-employment

Each case will be considered on its own facts, but is is reasonable to assume that a 'yes' answer to some of the following questions normally means that you are *self-employed:*

- Do you have overall control of the way the business is run?
- Do you offer your services to different individuals and organisations?
- Do you risk your own money in the business?
- Do you provide all the equipment that you use?
- Can you take on other people and pay them to help you out?
- Can you refuse to take on work?
- Do you work from home?

checklist for employees

Again, each case will be considered on its own facts, but is is reasonable to assume that if you can answer 'yes' to the following questions, you are normally considered to be an *employee*:

- Do you have to do the work yourself rather than hire someone else to do it?
- Does someone else control what you are doing?
- Are you paid for a period of time worked (eg day, week, month)?
- Are you entitled to sickness pay and holiday pay?
- Are you given set hours to work?
- Can you work overtime?
- Are you told where you have to work?

Of course, you can be an employee *and* self-employed at the same time. You might have a part-time job with an employer and also run a business from home.

If you work in a payroll office and are in any doubt about whether someone is an employee or self-employed, refer the matter to your supervisor. Cases which are unclear may eventually have to be referred to the Inland Revenue.

agency staff

Organisations sometimes take on agency staff for some functions, eg 'temps', cleaners and specialised staff. These people are not employees of the organisation where they actually carry out their work, they are employees of the agency and are paid by the agency, which will deal with their income tax and National Insurance payments.

There will be a contract between the agency and the 'client' (the organisation where the work is done) and payment will normally be made on invoice. The person carrying out the work has no involvement in this payment process.

CASE STUDY

EMPLOYEE OR NOT?

situation

Osborne Electronics Limited has a number of people working on its premises, including those listed below. Which of them would be on the company payroll?

Charles Osborne, Managing Director, founder of the family company, paid a salary monthly, given a company car.

John Less, office cleaner, provided by Kleenup Office Services who issue a monthly invoice to Osborne Electronics.

Hanif Patel, Production Manager, paid monthly.

Janine Green, production worker, paid weekly.

Mike Bright of Mike Bright Valet Services cleans the company vehicles from time-to-time. He issues monthly invoices for the work carried out.

Jimmy Osborne, son of the Managing Director, a University student, taken on in the Summer holidays to do temporary work, paid weekly.

Mark Sparks, electrician, called in occasionally to carry out maintenance work for Osborne Electronics. Paid on invoice.

answer

The following are on the payroll:

       Charles Osborne

       Hanif Patel

       Janine Green

       Jimmy Osborne

The following are self-employed:

       Mike Bright

       Mark Sparks

The following is an agency worker:

       John Less

CONTRACTS OF EMPLOYMENT

When an employee is taken on, the person processing the payroll will need:

- Personal details of the employee – name, details of how the money is to be paid (including bank/building society account), department, works number (if there is one).

- The rate of pay from the *Contract of Employment,* a written document setting out the employee's rights and responsibilities (see the next page). Under the Employment Rights Act 1996, employers must give employees a written statement of employment terms within two months of their starting employment.

CONTRACT OF EMPLOYMENT

Employer   Osborne Electronics Limited

Employee   Helen Elizabeth Cassidy

1 Continuous Employment
You are on a fixed contract of   2   years.
Your continuous service dates from   20 January 2000

2 Job Title
You are employed as   computer operator

3 Place of work
Your place of work is at   Head Office, 34 Raleigh Street, Mereford MR3 0JJ

4 Salary
The rate of your salary is   £15,000   per annum, paid monthly in arrears.

5 Hours of Work
Your normal hours of work are   35   hours a week, worked over a five day period (Mondays to Fridays inclusive).

6 Leave
You are entitled to   28   days paid holiday per annum in addition to statutory holidays. The leave is to be taken at a time convenient to the employer.

7 Sickness
Notification of absence should be made on the first day of sickness, in writing or by telephone. If you are absent for a period in excess of five working days, a doctor's certificate must be submitted to the employer. Regulations for payment during periods of sickness or injury may be inspected on request in the Administration Manager's Office.

8 Notice
The length of notice for termination of employment required from employer or employee is   4   weeks, subject to statutory requirements.

9 Grievance Procedure
In cases of dissatisfaction with disciplinary procedure you are to apply in the first instance to the Manager of the Sales Department. Details of the rules of the Company and disciplinary procedures may be obtained from the Administration Manager's Office.

10 Pension Scheme
Details of the contributory Company Pension Scheme, for which you are eligible, may be obtained from the Administration Manager's Office.

signed this 20th day of January 2000

C Osborne

C J Osborne, Managing Director and Company Secretary

H E Cassidy

Helen Elizabeth Cassidy

THE PAYROLL SYSTEM – AN OVERVIEW

The remainder of this book sets out the way in which the payroll system works in practice: the calculation of wages, the calculation of deductions from pay, paying the wages, making accounting entries and completing and sending returns to authorities such as the Inland Revenue. The diagram below illustrates this system. Study it carefully before reading on.

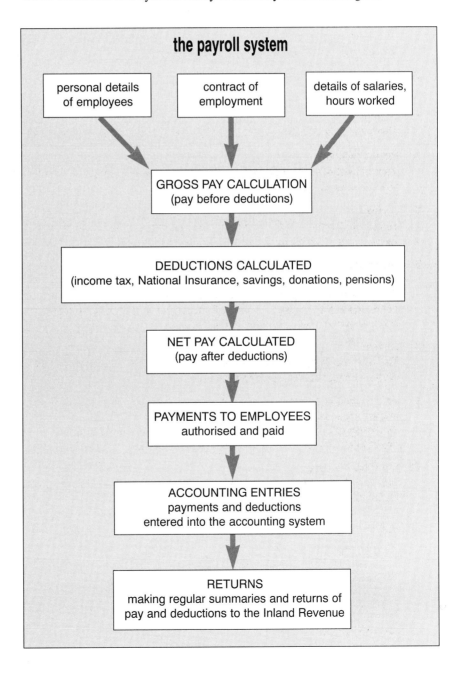

PAYROLL RECORD KEEPING

manual and computer records

Payroll records may either be maintained manually (on paper) or on a computer-based system. There are a number of commercially available computer systems such as Sage™. If a computer system is used it is essential that it has been approved by the Inland Revenue. You can normally assume that commercially available systems have been approved for use.

Any payroll system – manual or computer-based – must meet the needs of:

- the organisation's internal record keeping – its accounting system and employee records
- the employees – paying them promptly and accurately
- outside agencies to which returns have to be made, eg the Inland Revenue

Payroll records should be kept for a minimum of six years; some organisations keep them for longer periods. They should be filed in an organised way as they may be needed not only by the organisation but also by external auditors. They may also be the subject of inspection by the Inland Revenue and/or HM Customs & Excise (the VAT authorities).

accuracy

The accuracy of the payroll records is essential. Staff must be paid for work done and external authorities such as the Inland Revenue must be paid the correct amount. Input of information into the payroll system (eg hours worked, rates of pay) must be carefully checked and authorised.

security

The system must be organised to minimise the risk of information being corrupted or interfered with. Practical considerations include:

- information must not be processed without authorisation
- information must be checked, whether held manually or input into a computer system
- duties must be separated where possible – different people should carry out the various stages of payroll processing – if just one person did everything, fiddling the system would become easier

When computers are used, care must be taken that data does not fall into the wrong hands. Practical precautions include:

- ensuring that the payroll program has been exited when the computer is unattended, eg lunchtimes, so that passers-by cannot see confidential data

- changing computer passwords regularly (and not writing them down where they can be seen!)

Information held is additionally protected by the *Data Protection Act 1998* (due to replace the 1984 Act in 1999) which states that data held on computer and in paper-based files should be

- accurate and up-to-date
- maintained securely
- disclosed only to the person it involves and not normally to outsiders

timescales

The payroll system must be organised so that all activities are carried out promptly. The diagram on page 7 shows a typical payroll system which will be adapted to deal with the many varied ways in which people are paid, eg

- weekly or monthly
- by cash, by cheque or direct to the bank account

management of payroll

It is essential that responsibility for payroll is clearly defined within an organisation. In a small business the sole proprietor may be in charge; in a large organisation there may be a payroll manager. Some organisations may contract the payroll out to a bureau or firm of accountants. Whatever the system, it is important that payroll processing staff know to whom any queries or problems should be referred.

CHAPTER SUMMARY

- 'Payroll' is the term which describes a system which:

  - maintains employee details

  - records payments due

  - calculates pay and deductions

  - pays wages and salaries to employees

  - pays the deductions to the appropriate authorities

  - records the transactions in the accounting records

  - prepares and sends returns to authorities, eg to the Inland Revenue

- Self-employed people who work for an organisation are not put on the payroll. It is therefore important to distinguish between employed and self-employed staff.

- Agency staff used by an organisation are employed by the agency and not by the organisation.

- Employees are normally given a contract of employment which sets out, among other details, the pay or salary to be received.

- Payroll records may be maintained on paper (manual system) or on computer file.

- Payroll records must be maintained accurately and must be kept secure.

- Timescales for the administration of payroll must be strictly adhered to.

- The people who manage payroll in an organisation must be clearly identified and should be consulted in the case of queries and problems which cannot be resolved at a lower level.

KEY TERMS

employee	an individual employed by a person or organisation which places them on the payroll
self-employed	a person who has overall control of the business that he/she operates and is responsible for payment of income tax and National Insurance
agency	an organisation which employs staff which are contracted out to work for other organisations
employment contract	a written agreement between employer and employee, setting out the terms of employment – including the pay
Inland Revenue	the organisation which supervises and receives payment of income tax and National Insurance Contributions from individuals
HM Customs & Excise	the organisation which supervises and receives payment of Value Added Tax

STUDENT ACTIVITIES

further activities can be found in the Osborne *Payroll Accounting Workbook* **- please see the Introduction to this book for details.**

1.1 List five functions of a payroll system.

1.2 One of the advantages to a business of using a self-employed person is that the business will not have to pay National Insurance contributions in relation to the work done.

True or false?

1.3 One of the advantages of of a business employing a person is that the business will not have to deduct income tax from the employee's wages.

True or false?

1.4 State in each of the following cases whether the person described is likely to be employed or self-employed.

    (a) Olga works on the production line of a manufacturing company and regularly receives overtime payments.

    (b) Alice is the Managing Director of a company and has a company car.

    (c) Ramjit is a qualified accountant who employs five staff. He works for a number of clients. He operates from his own premises.

    (d) Sam is a marketing consultant, working from home She is working on a research project for you, but you do not stipulate her hours, or where she has to work.

    (e) Blake works in your accounts department and his salary is paid monthly to his bank account.

1.5 Maria is an experienced computer operator. She works for an agency and has been involved in a full-time project in your office for two months.

    (a) Who is her employer?

    (b) How is your organisation likely to have to pay for her services?

1.6 (a) Write down in your own words what a contract of employment is.

    (b) What type of information is likely to be included in a contract of employment? Write a list of numbered points.

1.7 Payroll systems must be operated on a computer.

True or false?

1.8 List three organisations which may need to consult the payroll records of a VAT-registered company.

1.9 All payroll records are covered by the Data Protection Act.

True or false?

1.10 Give two reasons why payroll payments should be authorised before they are made.

2 CALCULATING GROSS PAY

this chapter covers . . .

This chapter looks at how an employer calculates gross pay. 'Gross pay' is employees' pay before any deductions have been made. There are a number of different ways of calculating gross pay:

- a fixed rate for time worked – basic pay
- payment for extra hours worked – overtime, shift allowances
- bonuses and commission – extra payments based on productivity
- piecework – payment for the number of items produced

There are a number of ways of recording the amounts due, including time books, clock cards, time sheets and computer cards. These all form part of the authorisation process which is essential to the payroll system.

The amounts of gross pay calculated are sometimes 'coded' – they are used in the costing processes of the business.

NVQ PERFORMANCE CRITERIA COVERED

unit 3: RECORDING PAYROLL TRANSACTIONS

element 1

operate and maintain a payroll accounting system

❑ gross earnings are properly authorised, correctly calculated and coded

❑ records of gross employee earnings are correctly transferred to the payroll

❑ the organisation's procedures and timescales are observed

❑ discrepancies, unusual features or queries are identified and referred to the appropriate person or resolved

SOME DEFINITIONS

wages and salaries

The income a person receives from being employed is often referred to in terms of 'wages' or 'salary'. These can be defined as follows:

wages   payment made to employees normally working in the areas of production or service; payment is made weekly and is paid in cash or by transfer to a bank or building society account

salary   payment made to non-manual employees normally working in the areas of administration and management; payment is usually made monthly and paid directly into the employees' bank or building society accounts

gross pay and net pay

It is important to appreciate the difference between 'gross pay' and 'net pay'.

gross pay   wages or salary paid by the employer before deductions are made

net pay   the wages or salary actually received by the employee after compulsory and voluntary deductions

Note that employees normally speak about earning '£10,000 a year' (gross pay) but actually receiving '£700 a month' (net pay).

FIXED RATE PAYMENTS

Both wages and salary are *fixed rate* payments – the rate of pay is fixed in advance and is applied to the amount of time worked.

salaries

An annual salary is agreed between employer and employee and an equivalent amount is either paid in weekly or monthly amounts.

For example, Ramjit Singh, Production Manager, and Ellie Rose, Receptionist, have just agreed new rates of pay with their employer. Ramjit Singh is to receive £30,000 per year, Ellie Rose is to receive £13,000. Their gross (before deductions) income is as follows:

Ramjit Singh, monthly paid, will earn £30,000 ÷ 12 = £2,500 per month

Ellie Rose, weekly paid, will earn £13,000 ÷ 52 = £250 per week

wages

Wages are normally paid weekly. A payment rate for each hour worked is agreed and the employee will be paid according to the number of hours worked. A normal working week usually consists of five days, each of seven or eight working hours.

overtime and shift allowances

It is common with the fixed rate system to pay a higher rate of pay when an employee works overtime. Overtime is any time worked beyond what is normal for the working day, or time worked on a day not normally worked. Overtime can be worked by salaried staff and also 'wages' staff.

Shift allowances are extra payments given to staff who work unsocial hours because of the demands of shift working. For example a production worker who works from 12 noon to 8pm may be paid an extra £1 per hour for 6pm to 8pm, or he/she may receive an fixed payment of, say, £10 a week.

CASE STUDY

JIM BOX - FIXED RATE PAYMENTS

Jim Box, a storekeeper, is paid at the rate of £8.00 per hour for an eight hour day, five days a week. Overtime is paid at the rate of time and a quarter (ie 1.25 x £8.00) for weekday work and time and a half (ie 1.5 x £8.00) for weekend work. During one week Jim Box worked the following hours:

Monday	8 hours
Tuesday	9 hours
Wednesday	8 hours
Thursday	9 hours
Friday	8 hours
Saturday	4 hours

Jim's working hours for the week are therefore as follows:

Basic hourly rate 5 days x 8 hours	=	40 hours
Weekday overtime (Tuesday and Thursday)	=	2 hours
Weekend overtime (Saturday)	=	4 hours

Jim's gross pay for the week is worked out as follows:

Basic hourly rate (40 hours x £8.00)	=	£320.00
Weekday overtime (2 hours x £8.00 x 1.25)	=	£20.00
Weekend overtime (4 hours x £8.00 x 1.5)	=	£48.00
Gross pay for the week	=	£388.00

BONUS PAYMENTS

A *bonus scheme* is an incentive to employees to reach and exceed set targets, or to save time. For example, an employer may fix the amount of work to be completed in a certain time; if the work target is exceeded, bonus payments will be paid. The bonus payment will be paid either individually to each employee based on his or her performance, or paid as an average bonus to every employee based on the amount by which the target has been exceeded. The bonus, often referred to as a 'productivity bonus', can be paid either as a specific amount of money or as a percentage of the basic pay.

For example, if Jim Box, in addition to receiving the gross pay of £388 calculated in the Case Study, was awarded in that week a productivity bonus of 5% on basic pay, his gross pay will be increased by that bonus. The bonus is calculated (on basic pay) as follows:

Basic weekly pay (£320) x 5% (5/100)   =   £16.00

His gross pay will therefore be:

Basic pay	£320.00
Weekly overtime	£20.00
Weekend overtime	£48.00
Bonus	£16.00
Total pay	£404.00

Bonuses can also be discretionary, eg a Christmas bonus.

COMMISSION

Commission payments are normally made to employees engaged in selling goods. A salesperson receives commission on the sales that are made during a specific period. The commission is usually paid as a percentage of the total sales made. Commission could be paid in addition to a basic salary, or instead of a salary.

CASE STUDY

JOHN SPENDER AND HARRY WATT ON COMMISSION

John Spender, Area Sales Manager of a mail order company, receives a basic £750 per month salary plus commission at the rate of 5% on all the sales in his area. Harry Watt, working for the same organisation, sells direct to the customer and earns commission at the rate of 20% of his total sales.

During the past month:

• John Spender's area sales were £20,000

• Harry Watt's direct sales were £2,500

Their monthly pay is calculated as follows:

John Spender's pay = basic + commission

= basic + (total sales x commission rate)

= £750 + (£20,000 x 5%)

= £750 + £1,000

= £1,750 per month

Harry Watt's pay = commission only

= sales x commission rate

= £2,500 x 20%

= £500 per month

PIECE RATE PAYMENTS

Piece rate payment is another form of incentive to employees to work more quickly. The employer will agree a rate of pay for each article produced or operation completed and the employees will be paid only for the work that they have completed. Normally, however, there is an agreement between employer and employees that a minimum wage will be paid regardless of the work completed. An agreement of this nature is to provide the employee with a wage when the employer cannot provide work.

For example, Fred Parry and Helen Morse work at Lowe Electronics which produces electronic alarms. The employer and employees have come to an agreement that piecework rates will be paid as follows:

'Red alert' alarm	=	£2.00 per unit
'Klaxon' alarm	=	£1.50 per unit

The company has also agreed a minimum of £150 per week.

During one week Fred worked hard and produced 80 'Red alert' alarms whereas Helen Morse had a machine breakdown and only managed 40

'Klaxon' alarms. What are they paid?

Fred Parry: 80 x £2.00 = £160

Helen Morse: 40 x £1.50 = £60, but because of £150 agreed minimum wage, she will receive £150

AUTHORISATION PROCESS – RECORDS OF ATTENDANCE

An essential part of the payroll process is that all amounts due must be *authorised* before payment. In order to regularise the authorisation process it is important that all work done must be *documented* accurately and in line with the guidelines set down by the organisation. For staff paid on a time basis, a record of attendance must be kept. Employees' attendance records take a number of different forms which include the following:

- *time book* – a simple 'signing in' book

- *clock cards* – a card used in conjunction with a time 'clock'

- *time sheets* – records used by employees who work away from the premises

- *'swipe card'* – a card which records the hours on a computer activated by 'swiping' the card through a reader

time book

A 'time book' or 'signing on book' is often used in offices and is a simple ruled book in which staff enter against an allocated number:

- their time of arrival and departure

- their signature

clock cards

With this method, each employee who works regularly on the business premises has a clock card which is kept in a rack next to a time recorder clock. On arrival at work, the employee removes the card from the 'out section' of the rack and inserts the card into the time recorder clock, which stamps the arrival time on the card in the appropriate place. The card is then removed from the time recorder clock and placed in the 'in section' of the rack indicating that the employee is at work. When the employee leaves work, the card is stamped in the recorder clock and then placed in the 'out section' rack ready for when she or he works the next shift.

The clock cards are used to calculate weekly wages by the wages department of the business which will be able to see the actual hours worked by each employee.

In the example shown below, J Hicks works for Mereford Metal Castings as a lathe operator. He works a standard 40 hour week and is paid £8.00 per hour. He is paid time-and-a-half for overtime. His clock card for a typical working week appears below. Note that he has worked two hours overtime (on Tuesday and Thursday) and takes an hour for lunch each day when he 'clocks off' to go to the works canteen.

No.	701				
Name	J Hicks				
Week ending:	30 January 2000				
Day	In	Out	In	Out	TOTAL HOURS
M	0800	1230	1330	1700	8.00
Tu	0800	1230	1330	1800	9.00
W	0800	1230	1330	1700	8.00
Th	0800	1230	1330	1800	9.00
F	0800	1230	1330	1700	8.00
Total					42.00

	£
Ordinary time: 40 hrs @ £ 8.00	320.00
Overtime: 2 hrs @ £ 12.00	24.00
TOTAL GROSS WAGES	344.00

a clock card

time sheets

Time sheets are often used for employees who work away from the business premises on contract work, or for hourly paid staff who do not 'clock in' with clock cards. The employee completes his or her record of attendance on a specially prepared time sheet, indicating the hour of attendance each day. The foreman or supervisor in charge will normally check and sign the time sheet before it is passed for payroll processing. Illustrated on the next page is a typical time sheet. Note that time is split into three categories:

- time spent working

- time spent travelling

- time spent 'waiting' to do the job in hand, eg if a machine to be serviced is not immediately accessible to the travelling maintenance engineer

TIME SHEET (in hours)							
Name .... Works No: .... Week ending							
Job No.	Mon	Tues	Wed	Thu	Fri	Sat	Sun
Sub-total							
Travel							
Waiting							
Total							
Supervisor .... Date							

a time sheet

computer 'swipe' cards

Employers using this method require staff to carry computer cards to and from their place of work and to swipe the card in a computerised time clock on arrival or departure. This computerised system automatically records their hours of work.

This method of recording attendance is useful for businesses which operate a *flexitime* system. Flexitime is a method that allows staff to arrive at work when they like and leave when they like, provided they are present during a prescribed 'core' time (say, between 10 am and 4 pm). Staff will still need to complete the normal number of hours per week but can arrange their own hours of attendance. With this system, it is also possible to carry forward time worked in excess of the normal time or time owed to the company provided the amount does not exceed a set figure.

Using the computer card system for a flexitime system, the daily attendance hours are automatically calculated, totalled for the week and compared with the normal weekly figure. Wages for the week are worked out on the basis of the normal weekly figure.

COSTING AND CODING

The records described so far enable work done by employees to be recorded, the record to be authorised and used as a basis for payment of wages through the payroll system.

Organisations also use information about the time taken to carry out work as a basis for *costing:* they are able to calculate the labour cost of producing an item or providing a service. Costs can be allocated to various areas of expense – a product or class of product in the case of a manufacturer or a client in the case of a service.

The documents involved in this process include the time sheet and the job sheet. The *time sheet* (see page 19) shows the time spent by an individual on various different jobs, the *job sheet* shows the time devoted to a specific job.

The allocation of the hours to the product (or client) is carried out by means of a *code*, eg

- a job code (as shown in the left-hand column of the time sheet illustrated on page 19)

- a cost code (eg the client codes shown in the time sheet below)

Waring, Waring and Worne, Solicitors				**TIME SHEET**
Name Helen Maund			No. 96556	
Client	Code	Date	Hours	Work done
Osborne Ltd	4564	200100	1.5	Draft contract
J Hickman	6538	200100	2.0	Meeting

QUERIES AND ERRORS

If you work in a payroll office you will inevitably receive queries from employees about gross pay calculations, for example:

- rates of pay

- amounts of overtime worked

In each case you should investigate the possible error, consulting if necessary with the Personnel Department about rates of pay and hours worked. If there is a mistake, it should be rectified as soon as is practical. If, however, there is a potential dispute – for example, someone claiming that they should be paid at a higher rate – it should be referred to a higher authority. It may, for example have to be discussed with the employee's departmental manager. If in any doubt, refer to your supervisor.

CHAPTER SUMMARY

- Employers often pay their employees on a fixed rate – on a salaried basis or in the form of wages.

- Employees who work extra time or unsocial hours can receive extra pay in the form of overtime or shift allowances.

- Bonus schemes are operated by employers as a form of incentive to employees to be more productive. Bonuses can either be calculated on the basis of an individual's effort, or averaged out over a group of employees.

- Commission is normally paid on a percentage of sales in addition to basic salary.

- Piecework payments are made on the basis of the number of items produced and are a form of productivity incentive.

- Records of attendance are a part of the payroll recording and authorisation process; they include time books, clock cards, time sheets and computer 'swipe' cards.

- The payroll time records – which can be coded according to the work being done – are also used by the employer to work out the labour cost of specific jobs and products.

- Queries and errors relating to payroll records should be investigated promptly and referred to a higher authority where necessary.

KEY TERMS

gross pay	pay before deductions
net pay	pay after deductions
overtime	extra time worked by an employee, often at a higher rate of pay
shift allowance	an extra allowance paid for working a shift with unsocial hours
bonus payment	an extra 'bonus' payment normally calculated as a percentage of sales
commission	a payment which is calculated as a percentage of sales – a normal part of the payment package
piece rate payment	a payment which is based on the number of items processed by the employee

KEY TERMS	**time book**	a 'signing on' book used as a record of attendance
	clock card	a card inserted by an employee into the work's time clock to record attendance
	time sheet	a sheet completed by an employee recording the time spent on a number of jobs
	computer card	a plastic card inserted by an employee into a 'swipe machine' to record attendance on the employer's computer
	coding	the allocation of a specific number (or series of letters) to a job or client enabling the employer to record time (and money) spent on that job or client

STUDENT ACTIVITIES

further activities can be found in the Osborne *Payroll Accounting Workbook* - please see the Introduction to this book for details.

2.1 Calculate the *monthly* gross pay of the following employees:

	employee	annual salary
(a)	H Weston	£12,000
(b)	J Soper	£30,000
(c)	I Ramjani	£18,000
(d)	R Prosser	£7,800
(e)	J Osborne	£5,580

2.2 Calculate the *weekly* gross pay of the following employees:

	employee	annual salary
(a)	J Smith	£6,500
(b)	I Rose	£9,360
(c)	R Pellerini	£11,440
(d)	N Mutt	£6,760
(e)	R Singh	£7,800

2.3 Calculate the following employees' gross wages for the week, assuming that they are paid at an hourly rate of £6 for the first 40 hours and time-and-a-half for hours in excess of 40.

	Employee	Hours worked during week
(a)	Helen Marsh	35

(b)	Derek Hall	42
(c)	Eddie Bristow	48
(d)	Dilip Patel	50
(e)	Roger Draper	39

2.4   Mereford Sports manufactures up-market sports cars. At times of peak production the factory works six days a week (Monday to Saturday). The timing of the shifts and the allowances paid are as follows:

Shift 1	06.00 to 12.00	2 hours shift allowance
Shift 2	12.00 to 18.00	no shift allowance
Shift 3	18.00 to 24.00	6 hours shift allowance

The rates of pay are:

- an hourly rate of £7 for the basic 5 day week
- time and a half for working Saturdays
- shift allowance of £1 an hour (for all six days)

You are to calculate the weekly gross pay of an employee on each of the three shifts.

2.5   Annie Potts works for a bone china manufacturer. Her job is to decorate mugs on the production line. She is paid at a basic £6 per hour for a 40 hour week. As an incentive she also receives an additional weekly bonus of 50p for every mug decorated in excess of 150 a week.

Calculate her gross weekly wages for each of the following weeks:

	hours worked	mugs decorated
Week 1	30	120
Week 2	40	160
Week 3	38	175
Week 4	40	180

2.6   Healthy Life is a health products company which sells its goods direct to its customers in their own homes, usually through 'Healthy Life' parties. Healthy Life employes a number of area sales managers and sales representatives. Area sales managers are paid £18,000 a year, plus a commission of 1% of the total sales for their region. Sales representatives are paid on a commission only basis at a rate of 20% of the sales that they achieve.

During the first quarter of the year the four West Midlands Region reps recorded the following sales:

Sales representative	January (£)	February (£)	March (£)
John Mead	4,000	3,500	6,600
Rob Wallett	5,000	3,400	4,600
Joan Tilley	3,700	4,500	7,600
Guido Morioni	4,000	5,600	3,100

Calculate the monthly gross pay for Susanna Moore, the area sales manager, and for each of the four sales representatives for each of the three months.

3 PAY AS YOU EARN – INCOME TAX

this chapter covers . . .

This chapter starts by looking at the payslip in order to appreciate the various deductions made in the payroll process. It then concentrates on the calculation and deduction of income tax, in particular:

- the way Pay As You Earn (PAYE) works
- the division of the tax year into weeks and months
- the calculation of Free Pay (tax-free pay) through the personal allowance and tax codes, using Pay Adjustment tables issued by the Inland Revenue
- the way tax rates work
- the calculation of income tax using tax tables issued by the Inland Revenue
- the completion of deduction sheets for employees paid weekly and monthly – showing the weekly and monthly calculation of tax due

The chapter concludes by examining some of the ways in which the calculation of income tax can vary through the application of different tax codes.

NVQ PERFORMANCE CRITERIA COVERED

unit 3: RECORDING PAYROLL TRANSACTIONS

element 1

operate and maintain a payroll accounting system

❑ the current payroll status of employees is accurately recorded

❑ statutory and non-statutory deductions are correctly calculated and made in accordance with legal and organisational requirements

❑ the organisation's procedures and timescales are observed

DEDUCTIONS FROM PAY

gross pay and net pay

Gross pay is the total amount earned by an employee. It is the basic wage or salary plus any additional payments such as overtime and bonuses.

Net pay is the amount the employee receives after the employer has made certain deductions. There are a number of deductions an employer can make from gross pay. Some are *compulsory* and some are *voluntary,* as shown on the payslip illustrated below.

OSBORNE ELECTRONICS LTD		Pay Advice	Week 2
payments		**deductions**	
	£		£
Basic pay	180.00	Income tax	51.11
Overtime	80.00	National Insurance	25.45
Bonus	60.00	Superannuation	9.00
TOTAL GROSS PAY	320.00	SAYE	00.00
		TOTAL DEDUCTIONS	85.56
Gross pay to date	620.00		
Taxable pay to date	446.26	TOTAL NET PAY	234.44

Date	Employee	Code	Income tax to date	97.61
16.04.99	J Smithers	404L	National insurance to date	48.90

compulsory deductions

An employer must deduct two government taxes as and when they are due:

- income tax
- National Insurance contributions

Income tax and *National Insurance contributions* are both collected by the Inland Revenue.

voluntary deductions

An employer may deduct the following examples of voluntary deductions at the request of the employee:

- payments to charity by means of GAYE (Give As You Earn) – deducted *before* the tax calculations are made (not shown above)
- pensions (superannuation) scheme payments, deducted gross – ie *before* the tax calculations have been made
- SAYE (Save as You Earn) savings schemes, deducted *after* the tax calculations have been made

PAYE

what is PAYE?

Pay As You Earn, abbreviated and commonly referred to as *PAYE,* is the arrangement whereby an employer deducts income tax and National Insurance from an employee's gross pay on each pay day. This money is paid to the Inland Revenue by the employer who effectively *collects* the tax for the government. This is quite different from the regulations which apply to a self-employed person who has to settle up personally with the Inland Revenue, normally with a six-monthly payment.

the tax year

PAYE operates whether the employee is paid weekly, monthly or for any other tim period. The income tax and National Insurance collected is normally paid to the Inland Revenue monthly, but can be paid quarterly if the amounts are low.

Tax calculations are based on amounts due on earnings during the course of a 'tax' year. Tax matters have never been known for being simple – the tax year runs from April 6 in one year to April 5 in the next year. You would therefore refer to the '99/00' tax year (April 6 1999 to April 5 2000).

The tax year is divided into numbered tax 'weeks' and 'months.' These are:

Week	Period	Month	Period
1	6 April to 12 April	1	6 April to 5 May
2	13 April to 19 April	2	6 May to 5 June
3	20 April to 26 April	3	6 June to 5 July
4	27 April to 3 May	4	6 July to 5 August
5	4 May to 10 May	5	6 August to 5 September
6	11 May to 17 May	6	6 September to 5 October
7	18 May to 24 May	7	6 October to 5 November
8	25 May to 31 May	8	6 November to 5 December
9	1 June to 7 June	9	6 December to 5 January
10	8 June to 14 June	10	6 January to 5 February
11	15 June to 21 June	11	6 February to 5 March
12	22 June to 28 June	12	6 March to 5 April
	and so on . . .		

cumulative pay and tax

Any pay day – whether the employee is paid weekly or monthly – will therefore fall in a given tax week or tax month. This is important to appreciate because tax calculations are carried out by reference to the appropriate tax week or month. Calculation of tax through the PAYE system is normally carried out in what is known as a *cumulative* way, ie an employer works out how much tax an employee has to pay using the totals of pay and tax deducted *since the start of the tax year* (April 6).

If the payroll is processed manually, sets of tax tables produced by the Inland Revenue, will be used (see pages 31 and 32).

tax allowances

Income tax is a tax on the income received by an individual. 'Income' for tax purposes means wages and salaries, tips, bonuses, and benefits such as a company car.

Employees do not, fortunately, have to pay tax on all their income. In order to help the lower paid, the Government gives a *tax allowance* known as the *personal allowance*, an amount which can be earned during the tax year on which no tax is paid at all. This tax-free income is known as *Free Pay*.

The amount of the personal allowance varies, depending on factors such as whether employees are single or married, or over a certain age. Additional *tax allowances* are also available for items such as the purchase of special work clothing.

taxable income

Income which *is* liable to tax is known as *taxable income*. Taxable income is calculated by deducting the tax allowances (eg the personal allowance) from gross income. For any tax year therefore:

> *Taxable income = gross income minus the tax allowance*

The basic personal allowance, for example, for the tax year 1999/2000 is £4,335. With this allowance only income above £4,335 will be taxed.

TAX CODES AND TAX RATES

calculation of the tax code

How does the employer know what allowances have been given to the employee and how much tax to deduct? The Inland Revenue gives each employee a *tax code*, a number which is used by the employer to calculate the taxable pay. The tax code incorporates all the tax allowances, including the personal allowance, and is quoted *less the final digit*. The tax code for someone with a basic personal allowance in the 99/00 year would be 433L, ie £4,335 less the final digit plus the letter 'L'.

The range of letters which can follow (or precede) the number in the tax code is explained in detail on page 38.

tax code notification – Forms P6 and P9X

Tax code changes during the course of the tax year will be notified separately to the employer and to the employee by the Inland Revenue on *Form P6*. The employer should use this tax code when calculating payroll. The employee will undoubtedly check that the employer is applying the correct tax code by looking at the payslip (see page 25) which shows the code being used.

Tax codes also normally change at the beginning of each tax year (week 1 or month 1). The employer in this case is not sent a P6 for each employee but is notified about these changes in good time by the Inland Revenue on Form P9X (except for codes which end in 'T' or for 'K' or 'D' codes, for which a P6 will be issued).

income tax rates

The personal allowances and income tax rates used during a tax year are fixed in the government's previous *Budget*. The Budget – which also sets duties various items including drink and cigarettes – is announced before the beginning of the tax year and receives wide coverage in the media.

There are three rates of income tax applicable to various 'slices' of taxable income.

The figures quoted here apply to the 1999/2000 tax year.

- *Starting Rate Tax*: 10%, charged on the first £1,500 of taxable income
- *Basic Rate Tax*: 23%, charged on the remaining taxable income up to £28,000, ie on the next £26,500
- *Higher Rate Tax*: 40%, charged on taxable income over £28,000

If, therefore, you are fortunate to receive more than £28,000 of taxable income, you pay income tax at 10% on the first £1,500 and 23% on £26,500 and 40% on the excess.

Take for example an accounts assistant earning £15,000 a year and a finance director earning £40,000. How much tax do they have to pay during the tax year, and at what rates?

Assume they both receive the basic personal allowance. The calculations are as follows:

	accounts assistant		finance director	
	nearest £		*nearest £*	
Gross pay		15,000		40,000
Less personal allowance		4,335		4,335
Taxable pay		10,665		35,665
Income tax @ 10%	1,500 @ 10% =	150	1,500 @ 10% =	150
Income tax @ 23%	9,165 @ 23% =	2,108	26,500 @ 23% =	6,095
Income tax @ 40%		nil	7,665 @ 40% =	3,066
TOTAL INCOME TAX		2,258		9,311

TAX CALCULATIONS – PAYE

weekly and monthly calculations

So far in this chapter we have seen that an individual is given a *personal allowance* which is notified by the Inland Revenue by means of a *tax code*. That person is therefore entitled to earn so much a year as untaxed pay – *Free Pay*. He or she only pays tax on *taxable income*.

The sample calculations set out above are based on what a person earns each *year*. We will now look at how taxable pay is calculated each *week* or *month* through the PAYE system.

If a business uses a computer system to run its payroll, the software will automatically carry out the tax calculations. If a business has a manual payroll system, there are a number of calculations to be performed. The Inland Revenue issues booklets known as *tax tables* to employers to enable them to calculate tax and pay accurately. The two commonly used booklets are the *Pay Adjustment Tables* and the *Taxable Pay Tables*.

- **Pay Adjustment Tables** – these tell the employer week-by-week and month-by-month how much pay does not have to be taxed. This is *Free Pay*. This amount of Free Pay will vary according to the employee's tax code and the tax week or month reached. Clearly, as the tax year progresses the amount of Free Pay will increase week-by-week and month-by-month.

  There is a page for each tax week and a page for each tax month.

  Remember that *Gross Pay* (what the employee has actually earned in total) minus *Free Pay* (earnings that do not have to be taxed) equals *Taxable Pay* (earnings that do have to be taxed).

- **Taxable Pay Tables** – these tell the employer how much tax is due on the Taxable Pay. There are tables for each rate of tax.

The figures from these tables are recorded on a *deductions sheet* – a standard form (P11) issued by the Inland Revenue and the tax calculations are carried out on the deductions sheet, together with National Insurance calculations (which we will deal with in Chapter 4).

An extract from a P11 is shown below. It shows the side of the form, which records the income tax calculations. The reverse side (not shown here) records the National Insurance contributions (see page 52 for an illustration).

The only way to illustrate this process is by actually doing it. The Case Study which begins on page 33 shows how tax is calculated for two employees – one is paid weekly and one is paid monthly.

If you can, get hold of some tax tables and a P 11 deductions sheet and study them. Failing that, look at the illustrations on the next few pages. When you have done this, read the Case Study.

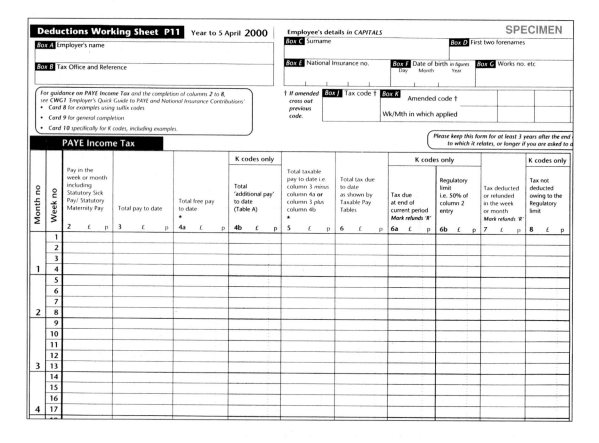

P11 Deductions Sheet (extract showing income tax columns)

TABLE A - PAY ADJUSTMENT

WEEK 1
Apr 6 to Apr 12

Code	Total pay adjustment to date £	Code	Total pay adjustment to date £	Code	Total pay adjustment to date £	Code	Total pay adjustment to date £	Code	Total pay adjustment to date £	Code	Total pay adjustment to date £	Code	Total pay adjustment to date £	Code	Total pay adjustment to date £	Code	Total pay adjustment to date £
0	NIL																
1	0.37	61	11.91	121	23.45	181	34.99	241	46.52	301	58.06	351	67.68	401	77.29	451	86.91
2	0.56	62	12.10	122	23.64	182	35.18	242	46.72	302	58.25	352	67.87	402	77.49	452	87.10
3	0.75	63	12.29	123	23.83	183	35.37	243	46.91	303	58.45	353	68.06	403	77.68	453	87.29
4	0.95	64	12.49	124	24.02	184	35.56	244	47.10	304	58.64	354	68.25	404	77.87	454	87.49
5	1.14	65	12.68	125	24.22	185	35.75	245	47.29	305	58.83	355	68.45	405	78.06	455	87.68
6	1.33	66	12.87	126	24.41	186	35.95	246	47.49	306	59.02	356	68.64	406	78.25	456	87.87
7	1.52	67	13.06	127	24.60	187	36.14	247	47.68	307	59.22	357	68.83	407	78.45	457	88.06
8	1.72	68	13.25	128	24.79	188	36.33	248	47.87	308	59.41	358	69.02	408	78.64	458	88.25
9	1.91	69	13.45	129	24.99	189	36.52	249	48.06	309	59.60	359	69.22	409	78.83	459	88.45
10	2.10	70	13.64	130	25.18	190	36.72	250	48.25	310	59.79	360	69.41	410	79.02	460	88.64
11	2.29	71	13.83	131	25.37	191	36.91	251	48.45	311	59.99	361	69.60	411	79.22	461	88.83
12	2.49	72	14.02	132	25.56	192	37.10	252	48.64	312	60.18	362	69.79	412	79.41	462	89.02
13	2.68	73	14.22	133	25.75	193	37.29	253	48.83	313	60.37	363	69.99	413	79.60	463	89.22
14	2.87	74	14.41	134	25.95	194	37.49	254	49.02	314	60.56	364	70.18	414	79.79	464	89.41
15	3.06	75	14.60	135	26.14	195	37.68	255	49.22	315	60.75	365	70.37	415	79.99	465	89.60
16	3.25	76	14.79	136	26.33	196	37.87	256	49.41	316	60.95	366	70.56	416	80.18	466	89.79
17	3.45	77	14.99	137	26.52	197	38.06	257	49.60	317	61.14	367	70.75	417	80.37	467	89.99
18	3.64	78	15.18	138	26.72	198	38.25	258	49.79	318	61.33	368	70.95	418	80.56	468	90.18
19	3.83	79	15.37	139	26.91	199	38.45	259	49.99	319	61.52	369	71.14	419	80.75	469	90.37
20	4.02	80	15.56	140	27.10	200	38.64	260	50.18	320	61.72	370	71.33	420	80.95	470	90.56
21	4.22	81	15.75	141	27.29	201	38.83	261	50.37	321	61.91	371	71.52	421	81.14	471	90.75
22	4.41	82	15.95	142	27.49	202	39.02	262	50.56	322	62.10	372	71.72	422	81.33	472	90.95
23	4.60	83	16.14	143	27.68	203	39.22	263	50.75	323	62.29	373	71.91	423	81.52	473	91.14
24	4.79	84	16.33	144	27.87	204	39.41	264	50.94	324	62.48	374	72.10	424	81.72	474	91.33
25	4.99	85	16.52	145	28.06	205	39.60	265	51.14	325	62.68	375	72.29	425	81.91	475	91.52
26	5.18	86	16.72	146	28.25	206	39.79	266	51.33	326	62.87	376	72.49	426	82.10	476	91.72
27	5.37	87	16.91	147	28.45	207	39.99	267	51.52	327	63.06	377	72.68	427	82.29	477	91.91
28	5.56	88	17.10	148	28.64	208	40.18	268	51.72	328	63.25	378	72.87	428	82.49	478	92.10
29	5.75	89	17.29	149	28.83	209	40.37	269	51.91	329	63.45	379	73.06	429	82.68	479	92.29
30	5.95	90	17.49	150	29.02	210	40.56	270	52.10	330	63.64	380	73.25	430	82.87	480	92.49
31	6.14	91	17.68	151	29.22	211	40.75	271	52.29	331	63.83	381	73.45	431	83.06	481	92.68
32	6.33	92	17.87	152	29.41	212	40.95	272	52.49	332	64.02	382	73.64	432	83.25	482	92.87
33	6.52	93	18.06	153	29.60	213	41.14	273	52.68	333	64.22	383	73.83	433	83.45	483	93.06
34	6.72	94	18.25	154	29.79	214	41.33	274	52.87	334	64.41	384	74.02	434	83.64	484	93.25
35	6.91	95	18.45	155	29.99	215	41.52	275	53.06	335	64.60	385	74.22	435	83.83	485	93.45
36	7.10	96	18.64	156	30.18	216	41.72	276	53.25	336	64.79	386	74.41	436	84.02	486	93.64
37	7.29	97	18.83	157	30.37	217	41.91	277	53.45	337	64.99	387	74.60	437	84.22	487	93.83
38	7.49	98	19.02	158	30.56	218	42.10	278	53.64	338	65.18	388	74.79	438	84.41	488	94.02
39	7.68	99	19.22	159	30.75	219	42.29	279	53.83	339	65.37	389	74.99	439	84.60	489	94.22
40	7.87	100	19.41	160	30.95	220	42.49	280	54.02	340	65.56	390	75.18	440	84.79	490	94.41
41	8.06	101	19.60	161	31.14	221	42.68	281	54.22	341	65.75	391	75.37	441	84.99	491	94.60
42	8.25	102	19.79	162	31.33	222	42.87	282	54.41	342	65.95	392	75.56	442	85.18	492	94.79
43	8.45	103	19.99	163	31.52	223	43.06	283	54.60	343	66.14	393	75.75	443	85.37	493	94.99
44	8.64	104	20.18	164	31.72	224	43.25	284	54.79	344	66.33	394	75.95	444	85.56	494	95.18
45	8.83	105	20.37	165	31.91	225	43.45	285	54.99	345	66.52	395	76.14	445	85.75	495	95.37
46	9.02	106	20.56	166	32.10	226	43.64	286	55.18	346	66.72	396	76.33	446	85.95	496	95.56
47	9.22	107	20.75	167	32.29	227	43.83	287	55.37	347	66.91	397	76.52	447	86.14	497	95.75
48	9.41	108	20.95	168	32.49	228	44.02	288	55.56	348	67.10	398	76.72	448	86.33	498	95.95
49	9.60	109	21.14	169	32.68	229	44.22	289	55.75	349	67.29	399	76.91	449	86.52	499	96.14
50	9.79	110	21.33	170	32.87	230	44.41	290	55.95	350	67.49	400	77.10	450	86.72	500	96.33
51	9.99	111	21.52	171	33.06	231	44.60	291	56.14								
52	10.18	112	21.72	172	33.25	232	44.79	292	56.33								
53	10.37	113	21.91	173	33.45	233	44.99	293	56.52								
54	10.56	114	22.10	174	33.64	234	45.18	294	56.72								
55	10.75	115	22.29	175	33.83	235	45.37	295	56.91								
56	10.95	116	22.49	176	34.02	236	45.56	296	57.10								
57	11.14	117	22.68	177	34.22	237	45.75	297	57.29								
58	11.33	118	22.87	178	34.41	238	45.95	298	57.49								
59	11.52	119	23.06	179	34.60	239	46.14	299	57.68								
60	11.72	120	23.25	180	34.79	240	46.33	300	57.87								

Pay adjustment where code exceeds 500

1. Where the code is in the range **501** to **1000** inclusive proceed as follows:
   a. Subtract **500** from the code and use the balance of the code to obtain a pay adjustment figure from the table above.
   b. Add this pay adjustment figure to the figure given in the box alongside to obtain the figure of total pay adjustment to date * **£ 96.16**
2. Where the code **exceeds 1000** follow the instructions on **page 2**.

Pay Adjustment Table for Week 1 of the tax year

SPECIMEN

Table B
(Tax at 23%)

Tax Due on Taxable Pay from £1 to £99

Total TAXABLE PAY to date £	Total TAX DUE to date £	Total TAXABLE PAY to date £	Total TAX DUE to date £
1	0.23	56	12.88
2	0.46	57	13.11
3	0.69	58	13.34
4	0.92	59	13.57
5	1.15	60	13.80
6	1.38	61	14.03
7	1.61	62	14.26
8	1.84	63	14.49
9	2.07	64	14.72
10	2.30	65	14.95
11	2.53	66	15.18
12	2.76	67	15.41
13	2.99	68	15.64
14	3.22	69	15.87
15	3.45	70	16.10
16	3.68	71	16.33
17	3.91	72	16.56
18	4.14	73	16.79
19	4.37	74	17.02
20	4.60	75	17.25
21	4.83	76	17.48
22	5.06	77	17.71
23	5.29	78	17.94
24	5.52	79	18.17
25	5.75	80	18.40
26	5.98	81	18.63
27	6.21	82	18.86
28	6.44	83	19.09
29	6.67	84	19.32
30	6.90	85	19.55
31	7.13	86	19.78
32	7.36	87	20.01
33	7.59	88	20.24
34	7.82	89	20.47
35	8.05	90	20.70
36	8.28	91	20.93
37	8.51	92	21.16
38	8.74	93	21.39
39	8.97	94	21.62
40	9.20	95	21.85
41	9.43	96	22.08
42	9.66	97	22.31
43	9.89	98	22.54
44	10.12	99	22.77
45	10.35		
46	10.58		
47	10.81		
48	11.04		
49	11.27		
50	11.50		
51	11.73		
52	11.96		
53	12.19		
54	12.42		
55	12.65		

Where the exact amount of taxable pay is not shown, add together the figures for two (or more) entries to make up the amount of taxable pay to the nearest £1 below

Tax Due on Taxable Pay from £100 to £26,100

Total TAXABLE PAY to date £	Total TAX DUE to date £	Total TAXABLE PAY to date £	Total TAX DUE to date £	Total TAXABLE PAY to date £	Total TAX DUE to date £	Total TAXABLE PAY to date £	Total TAX DUE to date £
100	23.00	6600	1518.00	13100	3013.00	19600	4508.00
200	46.00	6700	1541.00	13200	3036.00	19700	4531.00
300	69.00	6800	1564.00	13300	3059.00	19800	4554.00
400	92.00	6900	1587.00	13400	3082.00	19900	4577.00
500	115.00	7000	1610.00	13500	3105.00	20000	4600.00
600	138.00	7100	1633.00	13600	3128.00	20100	4623.00
700	161.00	7200	1656.00	13700	3151.00	20200	4646.00
800	184.00	7300	1679.00	13800	3174.00	20300	4669.00
900	207.00	7400	1702.00	13900	3197.00	20400	4692.00
1000	230.00	7500	1725.00	14000	3220.00	20500	4715.00
1100	253.00	7600	1748.00	14100	3243.00	20600	4738.00
1200	276.00	7700	1771.00	14200	3266.00	20700	4761.00
1300	299.00	7800	1794.00	14300	3289.00	20800	4784.00
1400	322.00	7900	1817.00	14400	3312.00	20900	4807.00
1500	345.00	8000	1840.00	14500	3335.00	21000	4830.00
1600	368.00	8100	1863.00	14600	3358.00	21100	4853.00
1700	391.00	8200	1886.00	14700	3381.00	21200	4876.00
1800	414.00	8300	1909.00	14800	3404.00	21300	4899.00
1900	437.00	8400	1932.00	14900	3427.00	21400	4922.00
2000	460.00	8500	1955.00	15000	3450.00	21500	4945.00
2100	483.00	8600	1978.00	15100	3473.00	21600	4968.00
2200	506.00	8700	2001.00	15200	3496.00	21700	4991.00
2300	529.00	8800	2024.00	15300	3519.00	21800	5014.00
2400	552.00	8900	2047.00	15400	3542.00	21900	5037.00
2500	575.00	9000	2070.00	15500	3565.00	22000	5060.00
2600	598.00	9100	2093.00	15600	3588.00	22100	5083.00
2700	621.00	9200	2116.00	15700	3611.00	22200	5106.00
2800	644.00	9300	2139.00	15800	3634.00	22300	5129.00
2900	667.00	9400	2162.00	15900	3657.00	22400	5152.00
3000	690.00	9500	2185.00	16000	3680.00	22500	5175.00
3100	713.00	9600	2208.00	16100	3703.00	22600	5198.00
3200	736.00	9700	2231.00	16200	3726.00	22700	5221.00
3300	759.00	9800	2254.00	16300	3749.00	22800	5244.00
3400	782.00	9900	2277.00	16400	3772.00	22900	5267.00
3500	805.00	10000	2300.00	16500	3795.00	23000	5290.00
3600	828.00	10100	2323.00	16600	3818.00	23100	5313.00
3700	851.00	10200	2346.00	16700	3841.00	23200	5336.00
3800	874.00	10300	2369.00	16800	3864.00	23300	5359.00
3900	897.00	10400	2392.00	16900	3887.00	23400	5382.00
4000	920.00	10500	2415.00	17000	3910.00	23500	5405.00
4100	943.00	10600	2438.00	17100	3933.00	23600	5428.00
4200	966.00	10700	2461.00	17200	3956.00	23700	5451.00
4300	989.00	10800	2484.00	17300	3979.00	23800	5474.00
4400	1012.00	10900	2507.00	17400	4002.00	23900	5497.00
4500	1035.00	11000	2530.00	17500	4025.00	24000	5520.00
4600	1058.00	11100	2553.00	17600	4048.00	24100	5543.00
4700	1081.00	11200	2576.00	17700	4071.00	24200	5566.00
4800	1104.00	11300	2599.00	17800	4094.00	24300	5589.00
4900	1127.00	11400	2622.00	17900	4117.00	24400	5612.00
5000	1150.00	11500	2645.00	18000	4140.00	24500	5635.00
5100	1173.00	11600	2668.00	18100	4163.00	24600	5658.00
5200	1196.00	11700	2691.00	18200	4186.00	24700	5681.00
5300	1219.00	11800	2714.00	18300	4209.00	24800	5704.00
5400	1242.00	11900	2737.00	18400	4232.00	24900	5727.00
5500	1265.00	12000	2760.00	18500	4255.00	25000	5750.00
5600	1288.00	12100	2783.00	18600	4278.00	25100	5773.00
5700	1311.00	12200	2806.00	18700	4301.00	25200	5796.00
5800	1334.00	12300	2829.00	18800	4324.00	25300	5819.00
5900	1357.00	12400	2852.00	18900	4347.00	25400	5842.00
6000	1380.00	12500	2875.00	19000	4370.00	25500	5865.00
6100	1403.00	12600	2898.00	19100	4393.00	25600	5888.00
6200	1426.00	12700	2921.00	19200	4416.00	25700	5911.00
6300	1449.00	12800	2944.00	19300	4439.00	25800	5934.00
6400	1472.00	12900	2967.00	19400	4462.00	25900	5957.00
6500	1495.00	13000	2990.00	19500	4485.00	26000	5980.00
						26100	6003.00

Taxable Pay Table B for 23% tax

CASE STUDY

EMPLOYEE 1: BILL BAKER – WEEKLY PAY

Bill Baker, aged 18, works as a trainee storekeeper at May's, a mail order company based in Mereford. His terms of employment are a 40 hour week at £6.00 per hour and a rate of time-and-a-half for overtime (ie £9 per hour). His employer uses a swipe card system for recording time worked. He is paid on a weekly basis. The Inland Revenue have advised May's that Bill's tax code for the tax year is 433L.

In the first two weeks of the tax year Bill worked the following hours:

week 1	40 hours normal rate
week 2	40 hours normal rate plus 8 hours at overtime rate

How does Bill's employer, May's, work out his take-home ('net') pay for the two weeks?

His employer has a number of basic documents to work from:

- The *computer printout* (produced from the use of the swipe card) showing the hours worked

- *P11 deductions sheet* on which to work out all the calculations for tax deductions from gross pay

- *Pay Adjustment Tables* showing the employer how much pay, depending on Bill's tax code, is not subject to Income Tax – this is the Free Pay

- *Taxable Pay Tables* showing the employer how much tax is payable on Bill's taxable income

The basis of the calculation is the P11 deduction sheet and we will show how, step-by-step, this will be completed with the Income Tax calculations. The form used in this Case Study for the sake of clarity shows only the columns you need for the basic tax calculations. An Inland Revenue P11 is much larger and also records National Insurance Contributions (see page 30).

Income Tax Calculations

Step one: calculate gross pay for week one
Establish how much gross pay Bill has earned:
Hours worked x rate per hour = gross pay
    40 x £6 = £240

Enter £240 in column 2 (pay for the week) of the deduction sheet
Enter £240 also in column 3 (total pay to date, ie £240)

Step two: calculate free pay to date
Calculate the free pay, ie untaxed pay, from the Pay Adjustment Tables on the page for week 1 (see page 31)
Locate Bill's tax code of 433 and read off total free pay of £83.45

Enter £83.45 in column 4a of the deduction sheet

Step three: calculate taxable pay to date
Deduct total free pay from the gross pay to date (column 3 minus column 4a)
In this case £240 less £83.45 = £156.55

Enter £156.55, the taxable pay, in column 5 of the deduction sheet

Step four: calculate tax due to date
Select Table B (tax at 23%) of the Taxable Pay Tables (see page 32), and find the tax
due on £156 (pence are ignored). As there is not a figure for taxable pay of £156 this
will be done by splitting £156 into £100 and £56, and adding up the tax due on these
two amounts, ie £23.00 plus £12.88 = £35.88. You can always check this on your
calculator: 23% of £156 is £35.88.

This figure, which shows tax at 23%, now has to be adjusted for the amount of taxable
pay taxed at 10%. This is done by deducting from it the figure shown in Table B
(Starting Rate Relief) on the right-hand page of the tax table under 'Weekly rates' for
week no. 1, ie £3.76: the calculation is £35.88 − £3.76 = £32.12.

Enter £32.12 in column 6 ('tax due to date') of the deduction sheet

As this is the first week at work for Bill, this 'tax due to date' is also the tax for week
one.

Enter £32.12 in column 7

Normally at this stage Bill's employer will work out his National Insurance
Contribution. We will explain National Insurance in Chapter 4. We will now see how
the Income Tax is worked out for Week 2, because the employer will need to base his
calculations on the figures for Week 1. The procedure is as follows:

Step one: calculate gross pay for Week 2

As Bill worked eight hours overtime in the second week his gross pay will be:

Normal rate:	40 hours x £6	=	£240
Overtime rate:	8 hours x £9	=	£72
Total gross pay		=	£312

Enter £312 in column 2 of the deduction sheet in the line for Week 2
Enter £312 + £240 (last week's pay) = £552, in column 3 ('Total pay to date')

Step two: calculate free pay to date (Week 2)

The figure will be obtained from the Pay Adjustment Table for Week 2. In this case,
free pay to date against Bill's code of 433L is £166.90. This is the amount of money
Bill has earned since he started on which he does not have to pay tax.

Enter £166.90 in column 4a of the deduction sheet

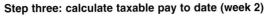

P11		Name: *William Baker*				Tax Code: *433L*	
Month no	Week no	Pay in the week or month 2	Total pay to date 3	Total Free Pay to date 4a	Total taxable pay to date (Column 3 minus 4a) 5	Total tax due to date 6	Tax deducted or refunded in the week or month 7
	1	240.00	240.00	83.45	156.55	32.12	32.12
	2	312.00	552.00	166.90	385.10	81.04	48.92
	3						
1	4						
	5						
	6						
	7						
2	8						

Step three: calculate taxable pay to date (week 2)
As in week one, deduct free pay to date from total pay to date (column 3 minus column 4a), i.e. £552.00 − £166.90 = £385.10

Enter £385.10 in column 5 of the deduction sheet

Step four: calculate tax due to date (week 2)
Select Table B (tax at 23%) of the Taxable Pay Tables, and find the tax due on £300 and £85 (pence are ignored): the tax at 23% is £69 plus £19.55 = £88.55. (Again check with your calculator: 23% of £385 = £88.55)
This figure of £88.55, which shows tax at 23%, now has to be adjusted for the amount of taxable pay taxed at 10%. This is done by deducting from it the figure shown in Table B (Starting Rate Relief) on the right-hand page of the tax table under 'Weekly rates' for week no. 2, ie £7.51: the calculation is £88.55 minus £7.51 = £81.04.

Enter £81.04 in column 6 ('tax due to date') of the deduction sheet

Note that this tax figure is not the tax that has to be paid in Week 2; it is the 'total due to date'; some of it will have been paid in Week 1.

Step five: calculate the tax due for Week 2
As £32.12 of the tax 'due to date' was paid in week one, tax for week two is calculated as follows:
Total tax due to date minus tax paid to date, ie £81.04 minus £32.12 = £48.92

Enter £48.92 in column 7 of the deduction sheet

As mentioned earlier, Bill's employer will also work out on the same deduction sheet his National Insurance Contributions on a weekly basis. It must be stressed that this calculation, explained in Chapter 4, is a completely separate process and is an additional deduction from Bill's gross earnings.

CASE STUDY

EMPLOYEE 2: HELGA SCHMIDT – MONTHLY PAY

Helga Schmidt is a Senior Sales Executive with Mays Mail Order. She earns £24,000 a year and is on the monthly payroll. She is also paid commission from time-to-time. Her tax code is 433L. Her earnings for the first two months of the tax year are:

April	Basic salary	£2,000
May	Basic salary + commission	£2,400

Income Tax Calculations

Step one: calculate gross pay for Month 1
This is £2,000 (£24,000 ÷ 12)

Enter £2,000 in column 2 of the deduction sheet within the Month 1 box.
Enter £2,000 also in column 3 (total pay to date).

Step two: calculate free pay to date
Calculate the free pay (ie untaxed pay) from the Pay Adjustment Tables for Month 1 (not illustrated). Locate Helga's tax code of 433 and read off total free pay of £361.59.

Enter £361.59 in column 4a of the deduction sheet

Step three: calculate taxable pay to date
Deduct total free pay from the gross pay to date (column 3 minus column 4a)
In this case £2,000 minus £361.59 = £1,638.41.

Enter £1,638.41, the taxable pay, in column 5 of the deduction sheet

Step four: calculate tax due to date
Select Table B (tax at 23%) of the Taxable Pay Tables (see page 32), and find the tax due on £1,638 (pence are ignored). As there is not a figure for taxable pay of £1,638 this will be done by splitting £1,638 into £1,600 and £38, and adding up the tax due on these two amounts, ie £368.00 plus £8.74 = £376.74. You can always check this on your calculator: 23% of £1,638 is £376.74.

This figure, which shows tax at 23%, now has to be adjusted for the amount of taxable pay taxed at 10%. This is done by deducting from it the figure shown in Table B (Starting Rate Relief) on the right-hand page of the tax table under 'Monthly rates' for Month no. 1, ie £16.25: the calculation is £376.74 – £16.25 = £360.49.

Enter £360.49 in column 6 ('tax due to date') of the deduction sheet

P11		Name: *Helga Schmidt*				Tax Code: *433L*	
Month no	**Week no**	Pay in the week or month 2	Total pay to date 3	Total Free Pay to date 4a	Total taxable pay to date (Column 3 minus 4a) 5	Total tax due to date 6	Tax deducted or refunded in the week or month 7
	1						
	2						
	3						
1	4	2000.00	2000.00	361.59	1638.41	360.49	360.49
	5						
	6						
	7						
2	8	2400.00	4400.00	723.18	3676.82	812.98	452.49

As this is the first month of the tax year, 'tax due to date' is also the tax for month 1.

Enter £360.49 in column 7

Normally at this stage the employer will work out the National Insurance Contribution for Month 1. In this Case Study we pass straight to the Month 2 tax calculation:

Step one: calculate gross pay for Month 2
The gross pay for Month 2 is basic salary of £2,000 plus £400 commission = £2,400.

Enter £2,400 in column 2 of the deduction sheet in the line for Month 2
Enter £2,400 plus £2,000 (last month's pay) = £4,400, in column 3 ('Total pay to date')

Step two: calculate free pay to date (Month 2)
The figure will be obtained from the Pay Adjustment Table for Month 2. In this case, free pay to date against a code of 433L is £723.18. This is the amount of tax-free money Helga has earned since the beginning of the tax year.

Enter £723.18 in column 4a of the deduction sheet

Step three: calculate taxable pay to date (Month 2)
As in Month 1, deduct free pay to date from total pay to date (column 3 minus column 4a), i.e. £4,400.00 − £723.18 = £3,676.82

Enter £3,676.82 in column 5 of the deduction sheet

Step four: calculate tax due to date (Month 2)

Select Table B (tax at 23%) of the Taxable Pay Tables, and find the tax due on £3,676 (pence are ignored). The figure will in this case need to be split into £3,600 (tax £828) and £76 (tax £17.48) giving a tax total of £845.48. Again, check with your calculator: 23% of £3,676 = £845.48.

This figure of £845.48, which shows tax at 23%, now has to be adjusted for the amount of taxable pay taxed at 10%. This is done by deducting from it the figure shown in Table B (Starting Rate Relief) on the right-hand page of the tax table under 'Monthly rates' for Month 2, ie £32.50: the calculation is £845.48 minus £32.50 = £812.98.

Enter £812.98 in column 6 ('tax due to date') of the deduction sheet

Note that this tax figure is not the tax that has to be paid in Month 2; it is the 'total due to date'; some of it will have been paid in Month 1.

Step five: calculate the tax due for Month 2

As £360.49 of the tax 'due to date' was paid in Month 1, tax for Month 2 is calculated as follows:

Total tax due to date minus tax paid to date, ie £812.98 minus £360.49 = £452.49

Enter £452.49 in column 7 of the deduction sheet

VARIATIONS IN CODES AND TAX RATES

The Case Study above shows the normal workings of the PAYE system for employees with standard tax codes. From time-to-time you will encounter variations in tax codes and tax rates.

So far we have used the commonly used personal allowance with a letter 'L' which follows it. This is an example of a tax code which has a letter following the numbers (*suffix* codes). The range of suffix codes is:

L = a code incorporating a single person's allowance

H = a code incorporating an extra allowance

J = a code incorporating an extra allowance, eg a married couple's allowance and where tax is at the lower rate

A = a code incorporating an extra allowance, eg a married couple's allowance and where tax is at the higher rate

P = a code where a person aged between 65 and 74 receives the single person's allowance

V = a code where a person aged between 65 and 74 also receives the married couple's allowance

Y = a code where a person aged 75 or over receives the higher age single persons's allowance

T = a code used generally

K codes

If the tax code is a number *preceded* by a letter 'K' it means that the taxable benefits of an employee (eg company car, mobile phone) and other untaxed sources of income are *greater* than the tax allowances given. The Inland Revenue issues rules on how to calculate the taxable 'cash equivalent' value of benefits in kind ('perks'). If a K code is issued, instead of being given Free Pay (income that does not have to be taxed) the employee has to pay extra tax on what is known as *Additional Pay*. This is best illustrated by an example:

Melanie Forster is a company director of Pavilion Limited and on the payroll of the company. She has the benefit of a company car and fuel paid for by the company; she also has untaxed income from a property she rents out – all of these are taxable, and are taxed through PAYE. The calculations are as follows:

Tax allowances in her code		Amounts she has to pay tax on	
Total tax allowances	4,500	Car benefit	3,500
		Car fuel benefit	1,500
		Property income	2,500
	4,500		7,500

Melanie's net tax allowance is therefore £7,500 (deductions) less £4,500 (allowances), ie *minus* £3,000. Her code is therefore K300 *(minus £3,000 with the last digit removed)*. In effect she has a *negative tax code*. What the Inland Revenue does through the K code is to add this negative amount of £3,000 to her annual earnings and tax her on the total. Suppose she earns £24,000 a year. Her taxable pay is:

Annual pay (salary)	£24,000
add negative amount	£3,000
equals taxable pay	£27,000

She is therefore taxed on £27,000, although her salary is £24,000. This is the reason why company cars and fuel paid for by the company are not quite the bonus that they might appear to be at first sight!

If you look at the P11 illustrated on the next page you will see that there are special columns for the calculation of tax for people with K codes.

How is the tax calculated? You should note that the appropriate page of the Pay Adjustment Tables is used for finding out the Additional Pay. The tables are therefore used for *adding* amounts to pay for people with K codes, just as they are used for *deducting* amounts when calculating taxable pay for people with normal 'suffix' codes such as 'L' codes.

The P11 form illustrated below shows the tax calculations for an employee earning £1,500 a month on a tax code of K200. In other words, he/she has £2,000 a year of benefits in excess of her allowances which is taxed in addition to her salary through PAYE. Note that:

- the *additional pay* in column 4b, taken from the Pay Adjustment Tables, is *added* to the gross pay to date in column 3 to give a taxable pay figure

- tax is calculated in the normal way from the taxable pay tables

- column 6b shows a figure which is 50% of gross pay – this is the *Statutory Limit*, the maximum amount of tax that can be paid that month; as it is more than the amount actually calculated, it has no effect

SPECIMEN

PAYE Income Tax

Month no	Week no	2 Pay in the week or month including Statutory Sick Pay/ Statutory Maternity Pay £ p	3 Total pay to date £ p	4a Total free pay to date £ p	K codes only 4b Total 'additional pay' to date (Table A) £ p	5 Total taxable pay to date i.e. column 3 minus column 4a or column 3 plus column 4b £ p	6 Total tax due to date as shown by Taxable Pay Tables £ p	K codes only 6a Tax due at end of current period Mark refunds 'R' £ p	Regulatory limit i.e. 50% of column 2 6b £ p	Tax deducted or refunded in the week or month Mark refunds 'R' 7 £ p	K codes only Tax not deducted owing to the Regulatory limit 8 £ p
	1										
	2										
	3										
1	4	1500 —	1500 —	–	167 42	1667·42	367 16	367 16	750 –	367 16	
	5										
	6										
	7										
2	8	1500 –	3000 –	–	334 84	3334·84	734 32	367 16	750 –	367 16	

A P11 completed for an employee with a 'K' code of K200

other tax codes

Other tax codes are mainly used when the employee has a second job or source of income. They include:

BR = a code where a person is taxed at the basic rate of income tax and has no tax free allowances (often because the tax allowances are being applied by the person's main employer)

0T = a code which indicates that all the person's income is taxable, as there are no tax-free allowances

NT = no tax at all is deducted at all – normally because the income level is very low and less than the Free Pay amount

D0 = all income is taxed at the higher rate of tax

changes in codes, refunds

It is possible that the Inland Revenue may change an employee's tax code during the tax year. For example, an employee may get married and be given the married persons allowance.

When a code changes, it will be noted on the P11 deduction sheet (a box is provided at the top of the form) and on the next pay day, it will be applied through the Free Pay calculations. It is possible, if the code is increased substantially, that the employee may be given a tax refund (marked 'R' on the P11, column 7). This may also happen when a tax code is issued after an employee has been on an 'emergency' coding – see below.

The cumulative nature of the PAYE system always ensures that tax unpaid or overpaid in any week or month 'comes out in the wash' and will be adjusted in subsequent weeks or months. Most employees should therefore finish up at the end of each tax year having paid the correct amount of tax.

'emergency' code and 'week 1/month 1'

Occasionally, if an employee starts work and has no tax code from the tax office, the employer will use the *'emergency' code* which will be the current basic personal allowance.

The emergency code is applied on a *week1/month 1* basis, which means that each tax week or month in the year is treated as the first tax week or month. The gross pay for each week or month is entered on the P11 as normal (column 2) but the Free Pay figure is taken each week or month from the Week 1 or Month 1 page of the Pay Adjustment Tables.

The effect is to take away the cumulative effect of PAYE. For example, if someone left school or college and started work for the first time in September (Month 6), the emergency code would mean that they are likely to have to start paying tax straightaway, and not get the benefit of the 6 month's tax allowance which would have accumulated since April. Free Pay for Month 1 would only be in the region of £360 (for people with the basic personal allowance) instead of over £2,000 for Month 6. Once, however, that the Inland Revenue issue a code to the employer (on a P6), normal PAYE procedures are carried out and the employee would eventually get a refund.

In the example shown on the next page, an employee starts work in Week 3. He (or she) has been

- placed on 'Week 1/Month 1' basis
- given a cumulative 433L code in week 5 (the basic personal allowance)

Note how tax is refunded in Week 5 (and marked with a letter 'R') and the amended code and week are noted in the box at the top of the P11. The old code should be crossed out in Week 5.

SPECIMEN

For guidance on PAYE Income Tax and the completion of columns 2 to 8,
see CWG1 'Employer's Quick Guide to PAYE and National Insurance Contributions'
• **Card 8** for examples using suffix codes
• **Card 9** for general completion
• **Card 10** specifically for K codes, including examples.

† *If amended* **Box J** Tax code † **Box K** Amended code † 433L
cross out ~~433L~~
previous ~~W1/M1~~
code. Wk/Mth in which applied W5

Please keep this form for at least 3 ye
to which it relates, or longer if

PAYE Income Tax

Month no	Week no	Pay in the week or month including Statutory Sick Pay/ Statutory Maternity Pay	Total pay to date	Total free pay to date	K codes only		Total taxable pay to date i.e. column 3 *minus* column 4a or column 3 *plus* column 4b	Total tax due to date as shown by Taxable Pay Tables	K codes only		
					Total 'additional pay' to date (Table A) *				Tax due at end of current period Mark refunds 'R'	Regulatory limit i.e. 50% of column 2 entry	Tax deducted or refunded in the week or month Mark refunds 'R'
		2 £ p	3 £ p	4a £ p	4b £ p		5 £ p	6 £ p	6a £ p	6b £ p	7 £ p
	1	–									
	2	–									
1	3	150 –	150 –	83·45	–		66·55	11 – 42			11 –42
	4	150 –	300 –	83·45	–		66·55	11 –42			11 –42
	5	150 –	450 –	417·25	–		32·75	3 – 20			R 19 –64
	6										

A P11 completed for an employee taxed on a 'Week 1/Month 1' basis until Week 5.
Note that in week 5 you should use the Starting Rate Table (see below).

which tax table?

The illustration on page 32 shows the Table B commonly used in payroll processing. It shows tax at the Basic Rate and is used in conjunction with the subtraction table for Starting Rate Relief. There are, however other tax tables for use when tax is to be deducted at other rates. The introduction printed in the Inland Revenue tax tables tell you which table is to be used and when. In brief, these tables are:

• **Table SR**

 This table calculates tax at the **S**tarting **R**ate.

• **Table B**

 This table calculates tax at **B**asic rate and adjusts for Starting Rate.

• **Table C**

 This table is used when the employee is to be taxed partly at Basic Rate and partly at Higher Rate (the Higher Rate part is calculated using Table D - see below). Table C already has the Starting Rate adjustment built in.

• **Table D**

 This table calculates tax at Higher Rate. It can be used in conjunction with Table C or for employees with code D0 (all taxable pay taxed at Higher Rate).

This may sound complicated, but once you are familiar with the layout of the tables and the way in which taxable pay can be split into different tax rates, the task of payroll processing is very straightforward.

- Gross pay is the total amount earned by an employee, net pay is the amount received after deductions have been made.

- Deductions are either compulsory or voluntary.

- Compulsory deductions include income tax and National Insurance contributions.

- Income tax and National Insurance are collected by the employer through a system known as Pay As You Earn (PAYE) which makes the deductions of pay weekly or monthly as the employee earns.

- The tax year runs from 6 April in one year until 5 April in the next and is divided into numbered tax weeks and tax months.

- Employees are given tax allowances – amounts of earnings which are free of tax.

- Taxable income is income on which tax has to be paid; it is gross income less the total tax allowance.

- The tax allowance of an employee is notified by the Inland Revenue by means of a tax code – the amount of the tax allowance less the final digit.

- Income tax is charged in 3 'bands': Starting Rate, Basic Rate and Higher Rate tax.

- For employers who process payroll manually, the Inland Revenue publishes Pay Adjustment Tables and Tax Tables to enable the employer to calculate tax due each week or month.

- If the payroll is processed manually the tax is calculated using an Inland Revenue form P11 – the deduction sheet.

- Tax allowances and codes vary according to the employee's circumstances: there are different codes according to marital status, age and level of income.

income tax	a tax, based on the level of an employee's income, collected by the Inland Revenue
National Insurance	a tax based on an employee's earnings, collected by the Inland Revenue
PAYE	Pay As You Earn is a cumulative tax collection system operated by employers on behalf of the Inland Revenue
tax year	6 April to 5 April
tax allowance	an amount of income earned by an employee on which tax does not have to be paid

tax code	a numeric code (plus a letter) which enables the employer to calculate the amount of tax due – it is the tax allowance less the final digit
Free Pay	the amount of money on which tax does not have to be paid
Additional Pay	the amount of money in addition to gross earnings on which tax has to be paid
Pay Adjustment Tables	Inland Revenue tables which indicate the amount of Free Pay or Additional Pay due on any given tax code on any tax week or month
Taxable Pay Tables	Inland Revenue tables showing the amount of tax due at Starting Rate, Basic Rate and Higher Rate income tax
K code	a tax code which indicates that the employee has taxable benefits in excess of tax allowances
emergency code	the basic personal allowance given by an employer when the employer has not yet been given the tax code by the Inland Revenue
week1/month 1	each tax week or month is treated as the first week or month in the tax year as far as the Pay Adjustment Tables are concerned

further activities can be found in the Osborne *Payroll Accounting Workbook* **- please see the Introduction to this book for details.**

STUDENT ACTIVITIES

3.1   (a)   Give two examples of compulsory deductions from gross pay.

(b)   Give two examples of voluntary deductions from gross pay.

3.2   In what week and in what month of the tax year are:

(a)   7 April

(b)   4 May

(c)   6 June

(d)   28 June

(Assume these dates are working days)

3.3   Explain what is meant by the statement 'PAYE normally works on a cumulative basis.'

3.4   A tax allowance is:

(a)   the income on which tax must be paid

(b)   the maximum amount of tax an employee is allowed to pay

(c)   an amount of income earned in the tax year which is not taxed

(d)   the amount of tax which should be paid during the tax year

Choose one of the above four statements.

3.5   Taxable income = ... minus ....
Complete the above sentence.

3.6   Free pay is:

(a)   total taxable pay received in a tax year

(b)   income on which income tax is not payable

(c)   taxable pay received in any tax week or tax month

(d)   income on which National Insurance contributions are not payable

Choose one of the above four statements.

3.7   How does the Inland Revenue convert a tax allowance into a tax code?

3.8   What is the form normally used by the Inland Revenue to notify changes in tax codes to the employer during the course of a tax year?

3.9   What are the current rates of

(a)   Starting Rate Tax

(b)   Basic Rate Tax

(c)   Higher Rate Tax

Include in your answer the 'band' of income to which these rates apply.

3.10 There are four employees on your payroll with a tax allowance of £4500.

Their annual earnings are:

Employee A	£6,000
Employee B	£14,000
Employee C	£27,000
Employee D	£40,000

When you have had the answer to 3.9 checked, use the figures to calculate the amount of tax each of these four employees will have to pay during the tax year.

3.11 Using your answer to 3.10, calculate the percentage (to the nearest %) of gross income paid out in income tax. Comment briefly on your findings.

3.12 What information do the following tax tables provide?

(a) Pay Adjustment Tables

(b) Taxable Pay Tables

3.13 What does a form P11 record?

3.14 Using the illustrations from the Pay Adjustment Table and the Taxable Pay Table on pages 31 and 32 of this chapter calculate the pay after deduction of income tax of the hospital employees listed below.

Assume in each case that the pay day is in the first week of the tax year and that the employees are paid weekly. The starting rate tax deduction figure for Week 1 is £3.76.

employee	*tax code*	*gross pay (£)*
R M Pitt	433L	250.00
N Doskopi	433L	275.00
N Trails	385H	450.00
N Emmer	375H	456.75
L Bowe	433L	195.00
M T Head	390H	305.00
Ray D Olligist	265H	380.00
N Jexion	433L	295.00

3.15 What is the tax code of the following two employees:

(a) D Smith

Total tax allowances £4,500

Amounts (apart from pay) which are to be taxed through PAYE: car benefit £4,000; fuel benefit £1,600

(b) T Patel

Total tax allowances £4,300

Amounts (apart from pay) which are to be taxed through PAYE: car benefit £3,000; fuel benefit £1,400, untaxed interest £1,750, property income £1,000

3.16 You are working in a firm's payroll office. What are the tax codes you would use if

(a) Naomi has her main job elsewhere and *all* of her income from your firm has to be taxed at Basic Rate.

(b) Bill's pay is *all* taxed at the higher rate of tax.

3.17 Which tax tables would be used for Naomi's and Bill's Tax calculations in 3.16?

3.18 (a) What is the emergency code and when is it used?

(b) How would it affect Sam, who has just started work for the first time in Tax Month 6?

(c) Will Sam lose out?

4 PAY AS YOU EARN – NATIONAL INSURANCE

this chapter covers . . .

The last chapter introduced the PAYE system and explained how income tax is deducted. In this chapter we turn to National Insurance and explain:

*   what National Insurance is
*   who pays it and at what rate
*   the way it is collected through the PAYE system
*   the alternative methods of calculation – using tables and percentages
*   recording National Insurance contributions on the P11 deduction sheet
*   some of the variations you may encounter when dealing with National Insurance

NVQ PERFORMANCE CRITERIA COVERED

unit 3: RECORDING PAYROLL TRANSACTIONS

element 1

operate and maintain a payroll accounting system

❑   the current payroll status of employees is accurately recorded

❑   statutory and non-statutory deductions are correctly calculated and made in accordance with legal and organisational requirements

❑   the organisation's procedures and timescales are observed

NATIONAL INSURANCE

National Insurance is a tax on earnings payable by employers, employees and self-employed people.

National Insurance (often abbreviated to NI) is used by the government to pay for state pensions and benefits such as unemployment benefit and income support. Payments of National Insurance are known as *National Insurance contributions*, often abbreviated to *NICS*.

payment of National Insurance

National Insurance is collected from employers and employees through the PAYE system; employers are legally responsible for these payments, which are made to the Inland Revenue (along with income tax collected – see page 107). Self-employed people, on the other hand, pay their contributions direct to the Inland Revenue and as an addition to their tax assessments.

The *Earnings* on which NICS are payable is not necessarily the same figure as the income total used for income tax calculations (there is no NI relief on pensions, for example). The Earnings include items such as pay, tips, bonuses and statutory sick pay and maternity pay. You should also note that NICS are not normally cumulative: the calculation for each week or month is taken in isolation – which is quite different from income tax calculation.

Everyone is given a National Insurance Number from the age of 16 and this number is quoted in all dealings with the tax office and the Contributions Agency. The 'number' is in fact a series of two letters, six numbers and a letter, eg AB 23 45 67 Z.

classes of National Insurance

There are a number of different types ('classes') of National Insurance. In this chapter we will be dealing exclusively with Class 1 National Insurance contributions paid by employees and employers.

Class 1	National Insurance contributions (NICS) paid by employers and employees
Class 1A	National Insurance paid by employers (but not employees) on company car and car fuel benefits
Class 2	Fixed National Insurance contributions paid by the self-employed
Class 3	Voluntary 'top-up' payments
Class 4	National Insurance payments paid by self-employed people on the profits that they make

CLASS 1 NATIONAL INSURANCE

All employees, except those under 16 and those over 60 (females) and over 65 (males) are liable to pay National Insurance. Class 1 National Insurance is payable by both *employer and employee* once a certain level of earnings has been reached. The figures quoted are the commonly used 'not contracted-out' figures for the 99/00 tax year:

employer   National Insurance is payable at a fixed rate of 12.2% when earnings exceed £83 a week or £361 a month (the *Earnings Threshold*) but only on the earnings over this amount. This limit is set at the same level as the personal allowance used in income tax calculations.

employee   National Insurance is payable at a fixed rate of 10 % when earnings exceed £66 a week or £286 a month – the *Lower Earnings Limit* – but only on the earnings over this amount. No National Insurance is payable by the employee on earnings over £500 a week or £2,167 a month (the *Upper Earnings Limit*).

Note from this that employees do *not* have to pay National Insurance:

• on earnings over the Upper Earnings Limit

• on company car benefits (Class 1A contributions)

Employers, however, do have to pay National Insurance on these amounts. This is one reason why employers favour part-timers and temporary workers – if their earnings are below the Earnings Threshold, they do not have to pay National Insurance. The diagram below illustrates the National Insurance contributions paid by employer and employee in the case of an employee earning an amount over the Upper Earnings Limit.

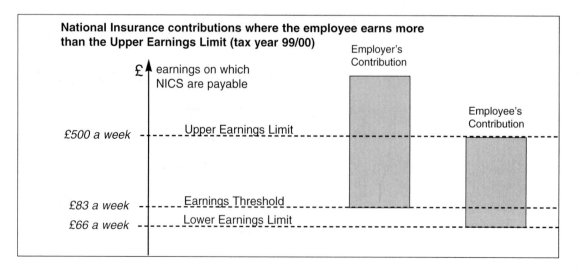

how much National Insurance?

There are two ways of working out how much National Insurance is due on an employee's earnings:

- using the National Insurance Tables produced by the Inland Revenue
- by calculating the amount using the exact percentage method

In both cases the figures produced will be entered by the employer each week (or month) on the NIC side of the P11 deduction sheet, illustrated below and explained on the next page.

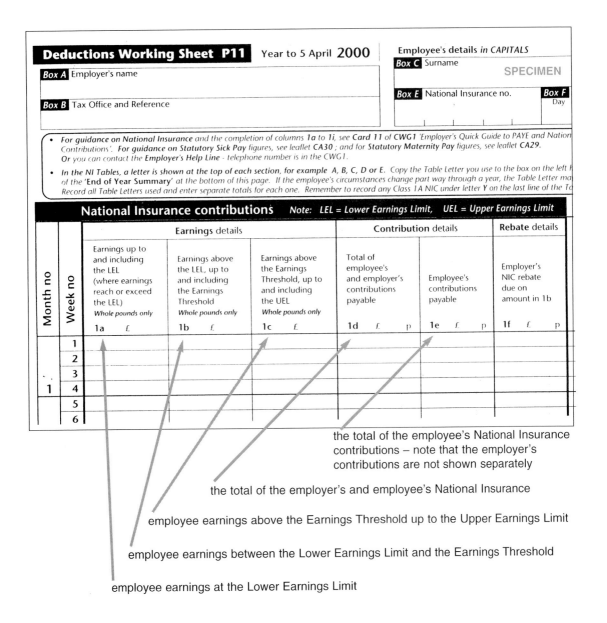

the total of the employee's National Insurance contributions – note that the employer's contributions are not shown separately

the total of the employer's and employee's National Insurance

employee earnings above the Earnings Threshold up to the Upper Earnings Limit

employee earnings between the Lower Earnings Limit and the Earnings Threshold

employee earnings at the Lower Earnings Limit

using the National Insurance Tables

The booklets produced by the Inland Revenue include a number of different tables, each with a different letter and set out on a weekly paid or monthly paid basis. Which should you use? There are a number of categories of National Insurance contributions:

- not contracted-out or contracted-out

- reduced rate or standard rate

You do not at this stage need to know all the possible combinations in detail, but it is worth noting that 'contracting out' refers to an employee paying into an independent pension scheme instead of the State earnings-related pension scheme – paying less National Insurance in fact. Reduced rate National Insurance, payable by certain married women or widows, is becoming increasingly rare.

The most common form of Class 1 National Insurance contribution – and the NIC used in the examples in this chapter – is the not contracted-out standard rate, set out on Table A, (illustrated on the opposite page).

You will see that completing the P11 with National Insurance contributions is very simple, all you have to do is:

1 Work out the weekly (or monthly) earnings - round the figure down to the nearest pound.

2 Locate this figure in the first column of Table A, making sure that you have used the weekly page for weekly pay or monthly page for monthly pay.

3 Read across the figures from the five columns from the left (1a, 1b,etc.)

4 Transfer the appropriate figures from these five columns of Table A to the same columns on the P11 (you will see that the column numbers and headings are the same). The process is shown on the illustrations on this and the opposite page – just follow the grey arrows.

You should also note that this procedure is the same every week (or month). National Insurance *is not cumulative*: there is a new calculation each week (or month) and the previous week's (month's) figures are not used.

The illustration on the left shows the P11 completed for weekly earnings of £100. Note that the P11 does not show the employer's contribution.

guidance on National Insurance *and the completion of columns 1a to 1i, see* **Card 11** *of* **CWG1** *'Employer's Quick Guide* tributions'. *For guidance on Statutory Sick Pay figures, see leaflet* **CA30** *; and for* **Statutory Maternity Pay** *figures, see* ou can contact the **Employer's Help Line** - *telephone number is in the CWG1.*

he **NI Tables**, a **letter** is shown at the top of each section, for example **A, B, C, D or E.** Copy the Table Letter you use t e **'End of Year Summary'** at the bottom of this page. If the employee's circumstances change part way through a yea rd all Table Letters used and enter separate totals for each one. Remember to record any Class 1A NIC under letter Y on

National Insurance contributions			Note: LEL = Lower Earnings Limit, UEL = Upper	
Earnings details			Contribution details	
Earnings up to and including the LEL (where earnings reach or exceed the LEL) Whole pounds only	Earnings above the LEL, up to and including the Earnings Threshold Whole pounds only	Earnings above the Earnings Threshold, up to and including the UEL Whole pounds only	Total of employee's and employer's contributions payable	Employee's contributions payable
1a £	1b £	1c £	1d £ p	1e £ p
66	17	17	5.58	3.45
			SPECIMEN	

| A | Contribution table letter | | | | | | Weekly table |

Employee's earnings up to and including the UEL	Earnings up to and including the LEL (where earnings reach or exceed the LEL) 1a	Earnings above the LEL, up to and including the Earnings Threshold 1b	Earnings above the Earnings Threshold, up to and including the UEL 1c	Total of employee's and employer's contributions payable 1d	Employee's contributions payable 1e	Employer's contributions
£	£	£	£	£ P	£ P	£ P
100	66	17	17	5.58	3.45	2.13
101	66	17	18	5.81	3.55	2.26
102	66	17	19	6.03	3.65	2.38
103	66	17	20	6.25	3.75	2.50
104	66	17	21	6.47	3.85	2.62
105	66	17	22	6.69	3.95	2.74
106	66	17	23	6.92	4.05	2.87
107	66	17	24	7.14	4.15	2.99
108	66	17	25	7.36	4.25	3.11
109	66	17	26	7.58	4.35	3.23
110	66	17	27	7.80	4.45	3.35
111	66	17	28	8.03	4.55	3.48
112	66	17	29	8.25	4.65	3.60
113	66	17	30	8.47	4.75	3.72
114	66	17	31	8.69	4.85	3.84
115	66	17	32	8.91	4.95	3.96
116	66	17	33	9.14	5.05	4.09
117	66	17	34	9.36	5.15	4.21
118	66	17	35	9.58	5.25	4.33
119	66	17	36	9.80	5.35	4.45
120	66	17	37	10.02	5.45	4.57
121	66	17	38	10.25	5.55	4.70
122	66	17	39	10.47	5.65	4.82
123	66	17	40	10.69	5.75	4.94
124	66	17	41	10.91	5.85	5.06
125	66	17	42	11.13	5.95	5.18
126	66	17	43	11.36	6.05	5.31
127	66	17	44	11.58	6.15	5.43
128	66	17	45	11.80	6.25	5.55
129	66	17	46	12.02	6.35	5.67
130	66	17	47	12.24	6.45	5.79
131	66	17	48	12.47	6.55	5.92
132	66	17	49	12.69	6.65	6.04
133	66	17	50	12.91	6.75	6.16
134	66	17	51	13.13	6.85	6.28
135	66	17	52	13.35	6.95	6.40
136	66	17	53	13.58	7.05	6.53
137	66	17	54	13.80	7.15	6.65
138	66	17	55	14.02	7.25	6.77
139	66	17	56	14.24	7.35	6.89
140	66	17	57	14.46	7.45	7.01
141	66	17	58	14.69	7.55	7.14
142	66	17	59	14.91	7.65	7.26
143	66	17	60	15.13	7.75	7.38
144	66	17	61	15.35	7.85	7.50
145	66	17	62	15.57	7.95	7.62
146	66	17	63	15.80	8.05	7.75
147	66	17	64	16.02	8.15	7.87
148	66	17	65	16.24	8.25	7.99
149	66	17	66	16.46	8.35	8.11
150	66	17	67	16.68	8.45	8.23
151	66	17	68	16.91	8.55	8.36
152	66	17	69	17.13	8.65	8.48
153	66	17	70	17.35	8.75	8.60
154	66	17	71	17.57	8.85	8.72
155	66	17	72	17.79	8.95	8.84
156	66	17	73	18.02	9.05	8.97
157	66	17	74	18.24	9.15	9.09
158	66	17	75	18.46	9.25	9.21
159	66	17	76	18.68	9.35	9.33

using the the exact percentage method

Another way of calculating Class 1 National Insurance contributions (NICS) is to work out the contributions as a *set percentage* of weekly or monthly earnings. The percentages for the tax year 1999/2000 are as follows:

NOT CONTRACTED-OUT CONTRIBUTIONS		
Total weekly earnings	**Employee pays**	**Employer pays**
Up to £66	Nil	Nil
£66.01 to £83	10% on earnings between £66 and £500	Nil
£83.01 to £500		12.2%
over £500	10% on £434	12.2%

The calculations are performed as shown below. Remember that NICS are only due if the employee's earnings exceed the Lower Earnings Limit.

employee contribution

This is the difference between the Upper Earnings Limit and the Lower Earnings Limit at the 10% percentage rate (rounded to the nearest penny). Note that figures coming to exactly half a penny are rounded *down*. For Table A there is a minimum contribution of 1p for earnings between 1p and 5p above the Lower Earnings Limit.

Note that no National Insurance has to be paid by the employee for earnings over the Upper Earnings Limit.

employer contribution

Calculate the amount due on *all* the employee's earnings above the earnings (PAYE) threshold using the 12.2% percentage rate (the percentage in the right-hand column of the table set out above). Therefore if the earnings are £450 a week, the employer pays:

£450 less £83	=	£367
£367 x 12.2%	=	£44.77

Figures should be rounded to the nearest penny and figures coming to exactly half a penny are rounded *down*.

The Case Study which follows shows how National Insurance is calculated using the set percentage method. You will see from the complexity of the calculations why the published Tables are useful to employers!

OSBORNE ELECTRONICS – CALCULATING NICS

Jessie Howe is a new member of staff in the payroll section of Osborne Electronics. As a training exercise her supervisor asks her to work out the Class 1 National Insurance contributions (NICS) of a number of weekly paid staff using the exact percentage method (using the same rates as shown on the previous page.)

The staff and their pay are:

Jim Trimble	weekly pay of £61
Ken Stanmore	weekly pay of £105
Helen Donat	weekly pay of £665

calculations: Jim Trimble – weekly pay £61

employee's contribution and employer's contribution
NIL   (the weekly pay is below the Lower Earnings Limit)

calculations: Ken Stanmore – weekly pay £105

employee's contribution
10% x £39 (ie £105 minus £66)   =   £3.90

employer's contribution
12.2% x £22 (ie £105 minus £83)   =   £2.68

TOTAL NATIONAL INSURANCE PAYABLE   £6.58

calculations: Helen Donat – weekly pay £665

employee's contribution
10% x £434 (ie £500 minus £66)   =   £43.40

employer's contribution
12.2% x £582 (ie £665 minus £83)   =   £71.00

TOTAL NATIONAL INSURANCE PAYABLE   £114.40

EARNINGS OVER THE UPPER EARNINGS LIMIT

As we have already seen, if an employee's earnings are greater than the upper earnings limit, the *employee* does not have to pay any NICS (contributions) on the earnings over the limit. The *employer,* however, does. The employer's contribution may be calculated by the percentage method, or it may be worked out using the *Additional Gross Pay Table* at the end of the published Tables. If the tables are used, the employer

- subtracts the upper earnings limit from the total gross pay to give the earnings on which the employer alone has to pay contributions

- uses the Additional Gross Pay Table to work out the extra contribution due

- adds this figure to the maximum employer's contribution figure shown in the main table to provide the employer's total contribution

NOT CONTRACTED-OUT TABLES B AND C

So far in this chapter we have concentrated on the most common form of National Insurance Contribution – the not contracted-out standard rate contribution. This can be worked out using either the published Tables, or by using the set percentage method. If you deal with payroll you may well encounter other contribution rates and have to use the other two tables in the not contracted-out booklet – Table B and Table C, or use Tables C, D, E, F, G and S for contracted-out contributions.

Table B is used for married women or widows who have the right to pay not contracted-out contributions at a *reduced rate*. The employer must hold certificates CA4139, CF383 or CF380A to authorise this lower rate.

Table C is used is used for employees who have reached the state pension age: 60 for women or 65 for men. In this case contributions are paid only by the employer and not by the employee. A certificate CA4140, CF381 or CF384 must be held. Table C is also used for employees who have Certificate CA2700 for deferred payment of NICS.

CONTRACTED-OUT NATIONAL INSURANCE

An employee may *contract out* from paying into the standard state pension schemes and instead pay into a *contracted-out* company pension scheme organised by the employer, or into a *contracted-out* personal pension scheme run by a financial services company. As the employee will not get the full benefit of the state pensions, a lower rate of National Insurance Contribution is payable through PAYE if the scheme is a *company* pension scheme. As with not contracted-out contributions, the employer can either use the percentage calculation method or refer to National Insurance tables (for example Tables D and E).

Both employee and employer pay a reduced rate on *earnings between the lower and upper earnings limits*. For example the reductions for Table D are: employee 1.6%, and employer 3%. As there is no employer National Insurance contribution for earnings between the Lower Earnings Limit and the Earnings Threshold (see diagram on page 50) the employer gets a rebate for earnings between these two amounts. For Table D this is 3% of £17 (£83 minus £66) which is 51p. Employers must hold a valid certificate from the Contributions Agency to apply the contracted-out rates.

Note that if it is a *personal pension scheme* that is contracted-out, the employer uses the normal not contracted-out National Insurance rates and the DSS deals direct with the pension provider to provide the benefits for the policy holder.

DIRECTORS' NATIONAL INSURANCE

National Insurance is normally *not cumulative* – the earnings for each week or month are treated separately and as and when they are received. Highly-paid employees therefore benefit from only paying contributions up to the amount of the Upper Earnings Limit. They can earn substantial sums in excess of this amount and pay no National Insurance on the excess.

What, then, is to stop owners of businesses from paying themselves in one or two large lump sums during the course of the tax year? The income tax would be paid as due because the PAYE system would apply the appropriate amount of Free Pay. In principle they could avoid paying a large amount of National Insurance. The Inland Revenue, in a move to prevent this form of evasion has introduced a cumulative Directors' National Insurance Scheme.

You do not need to know how this works in detail, but you should be aware that each time directors are paid, you calculate National Insurance contributions on the *total* pay in the tax year to date and deduct any National Insurance paid to date – ie the system becomes *cumulative*. There is also a scheme whereby directors can be treated similarly to other employees during the tax year with a balancing adjustment at the end of the year to comply with the cumulative basis.

CHAPTER SUMMARY

KEY TERMS

- National Insurance is a tax on earnings paid by employers, employees and self-employed people.

- Collection of National Insurance is the responsibility of the Inland Revenue.

- National Insurance is divided into a number of 'classes' – Class 1 National Insurance is paid by people on an employer's payroll and also by the employer through the PAYE system.

- Class 1 National Insurance is only payable once an employee's pay has reached a certain weekly or monthly money amount – the Lower Earnings Limit.

- The employee pays National Insurance on earnings between the Lower and Upper Earnings Limits, the employer pays National Insurance on earnings over the PAYE Earnings Threshold.

- National Insurance contributions, unlike income tax, are not cumulative – each week or month is taxed separately and no adjustments have to be made for previous weeks or months.

- National Insurance contributions may be calculated either by using Tables prepared by the Inland Revenue or just by using a calculator and applying the set percentage method.

- Form P11 – the standard deductions sheet – is used to record National Insurance contributions which are paid to the Inland Revenue along with income tax collected.

NICS	**N**ational **I**nsurance **C**ontributions paid
National Insurance number	a unique identification code given to people over 16 and used by the tax authorities, eg AB 234567 Z
Class 1 National Insurance	the type of National Insurance paid by employees and employers
Lower Earnings Limit	the amount up to which an employee can earn each week or month without the employee or employer having to pay National Insurance
Upper Earnings Limit	the amount of earnings an employee can earn each week or month over which the employee (but not the employer) does not have to pay any National Insurance
Earnings Threshold	the amount up to which an employee can earn each week or month without the employer having to pay National Insurance
Contracted-out employees	employees who pay a lower rate of National Insurance because they pay into a company contracted-out pension scheme and will not receive the state earnings-related pension

further activities can be found in the Osborne *Payroll Accounting Workbook* - please see the Introduction to this book for details.

STUDENT ACTIVITIES

4.1 Class 1 National Insurance is only paid by employees.
True or false?

4.2 How is Class 1 National Insurance collected?

4.3 National Insurance is the direct responsibility of
(a) The Department of Trade and Industry
(b) The Inland Revenue
(c) The Chartered Insurers Institute
(d) HM Customs & Excise

Choose *one* option from the above.

4.4 Draw up five columns on a sheet of paper and head them 1a, 1b, 1c, 1d and 1e (as you would find on a P11).

Using Table A on page 53, set out the weekly National Insurance contributions for the following weekly earnings for an employee (remember to use the nearest figure *below* the weekly earnings amount:

Week 1	earnings of £130.25
Week 2	earnings of £130.95
Week 3	earnings of £147.85
Week 4	earnings of £153.25
Week 5	earnings of £155.92
Week 6	earnings of £158.95

4.5 Using the set percentage table on page 54, calculate the employer's and employee's contributions for the following weekly-paid employees:

(a)	Jo Graham	£50
(b)	Jim Mortimer	£80
(c)	Rashid Singh	£100
(d)	Tanya Smith	£270
(e)	John Moore	£376
(f)	Helen O'Troy	£200
(g)	Kevin Murdoch	£600
(h)	Sam Baxter	£850

FURTHER ASPECTS OF PAY AS YOU EARN

this chapter covers . . .

The last two chapters have covered the two compulsory deductions from gross pay – income tax and National Insurance. In this chapter we look at voluntary deductions from gross pay :

- pension contributions
- Save As You Earn (SAYE) – savings payments made through the employer
- Give As You Earn (GAYE) – giving to charities through the employer

We also look at some further aspects of pay and PAYE:

- holiday pay – how much pay and when should it be paid?
- profit-related pay – tax relief given on extra pay based on the employer's profits
- advances of pay – payment of wages or salaries made in advance
- statutory sick pay and statutory maternity pay

NVQ PERFORMANCE CRITERIA COVERED

unit 3: RECORDING PAYROLL TRANSACTIONS

element 1

operate and maintain a payroll accounting system

- ❏ the current payroll status of employees is accurately recorded
- ❏ statutory and non-statutory deductions are correctly calculated and made in accordance with legal and organisational requirements
- ❏ the organisation's procedures and timescales are observed

TYPES OF PENSION

Before learning about the deductions made from pay for pension contributions it is important to have a clear idea about the different types of pension scheme and how they are paid for by the employee.

state retirement pension

The state retirement pension provides a basic pension from the age of 65 (men) or 60 (women) under present ruling. For those who are worried that this unfairly discriminates against men, the age limits will eventually even out at 65 – in 2020!

To obtain the full pension the employee must have contributed NICS for about 90% of his or her working life (39 years for a woman, 44 years for a man). For the employee who has not contributed the required amount, a reduced pension is available.

State Earnings Related Pension Scheme (SERPS)

This additional state scheme provides a pension which is related to an employee's earnings over his or her working life; the scheme is funded from National Insurance contributions. SERPS is available to any employee, unless that person has 'contracted out' to pay into a company scheme or private scheme (see below). In other words, anyone who has paid not contracted-out NICS is eligible for SERPS.

This may not turn out to be as attractive as you might think: when SERPS was first introduced it aimed to provide a pension of up to 25% of a person's earnings. SERPS has now been substantially reduced in value: benefits are gradually being reduced by successive governments which are encouraging the growth of private (ie non-state) pension schemes.

Remember that both state schemes are paid for from National Insurance contributions paid by employers and employees. It is interesting to note that there is no 'pot of money' set aside for this system – this year's pensioners are paid from this year's contributions. As more people retire than ever before, there is an ever-increasing demand on National Insurance payments. The present government is carrying out a thorough review of pension provision – so it is very much a case of 'watch this space.'

company schemes – occupational pensions

Many employees belong to *occupational pension* (superannuation) schemes, often called *company schemes*. These are pension schemes organised by the employer – the employee normally pays a percentage of salary and the employer additionally tops up the payment. Some employers pay *all* the contributions as an employee perk. The money is paid into an investment fund which is managed either by the employer or by an independent financial services company. There are two basic types of company scheme:

- *defined benefit scheme*
  This is where the amount of the pension is related to the number of years worked by the employee and the final salary. Employees can 'buy' extra years to boost the final pension.

- *money-purchase scheme (defined contribution scheme)*
  This is where the contributions are paid into a fund managed by a financial services company; on retirement the funds that have accumulated are used to buy pension benefits, eg an annuity (a series of set payments made until the retired person dies).

As you can see, there is an element of *risk* in company pension schemes:

- if the funds are managed by the company, the company may illegally dip into them and spend them (as happened in the notorious Maxwell affair)
- if the funds are managed by a financial services company, the value of the final pension will depend on the company's investment performance

The Pensions Act 1995 was passed to help protect people's pensions against the illegal pilfering of pension funds.

company schemes – AVCs

Employees are allowed to contribute a set percentage of their earnings (currently 15%) to a company scheme and to set the contributions against tax – in other words the pension contribution is deducted from pay before the tax calculation is made. If the contribution is less than 15% (it often is) then the employee is allowed to make an *additional voluntary contribution* (AVC) to make the contribution up to 15% of pay. This has the double advantage of helping to boost the amount of the pension and also to save tax. Employees can also pay AVCs up to the 15% limit into a separate fund operated by a financial services company – this is a *free-standing additional voluntary contribution* (FSAVC) and as a private arrangement has no effect on payroll at all.

private pension plans

Private pension plans – *personal pensions* – are available to employees and also to the self-employed. Private pension plans are operated by financial services companies; the amount eventually received as a pension depends on the amount paid into the scheme and the success of the financial services company. Between 17.5% and 40% of earnings can be paid into a private pension plan, the percentage depending on age. Contributions can be made by the employer (by arrangement) and the employee. The advantage of these schemes is that they are 'portable' – they do not have to be changed if the employee changes job. Also the contributions attract tax relief. Employees obtain tax relief by paying the premium net of basic rate tax. If the employee is a higher rate tax payer further relief is given on the employee's tax code.

PENSION CONTRIBUTIONS AND PAYROLL

Look at the table below to see how National Insurance contributions and income tax are affected by the type of pension an employee has. If you are working out payroll the main questions you should ask are:

1   Is the employee contracted-out for National Insurance purposes?

2   Is the pension payment deducted before or after income tax is deducted from gross pay?

pension scheme	how it works	National Insurance and the P11	income tax and the P11
state retirement pension	state scheme available to employees who have made NICS	NI calculated in the normal way – this *is* the contribution. Entered on P11.	No effect on tax calculation
State Earnings-Related Pension Scheme (SERPS)	state scheme available to employees who have made NICS on a not contracted-out basis	NI calculated at the not contracted-out rate – this *is* the contribution. Entered on P11.	No effect on tax calculation
company schemes	contributions made by employer and employee (or just employer) into a fund operated by the company or a financial services company – up to 15% of pay	NI calculated at the contracted-out rate for approved schemes (a certificate must be held). Entered on P11.	Contributions deducted from gross pay *before* tax is calculated – the net figure goes on the P11 as 'pay for week or month'
Additional Voluntary Contributions (AVCs)	additional contributions made by an employee into a fund operated by the company or a financial services company to bring the contribution up to 15% of pay	NI calculated at the contracted-out rate for approved schemes. Entered on P11.	Contributions deducted from gross pay *before* tax is calculated – the net figure goes on the P11 as 'pay for week or month'
private pension plans	Contributions made by employees/employer into a fund operated by a financial services company – a fully 'portable' pension	NI calculated at the *not* contracted-out rate. Entered on P11. NI not payable on the employer's contribution (by arrangement)	Contributions deducted *after* the tax calculation has been made – from net pay. The P11 is not affected in any way

SAVE AS YOU EARN (SAYE)

Save As You Earn (SAYE), also known as Sharesave, is a government-instituted savings scheme operated by employers. It deducts savings payments from the *net* pay of employees and pays them direct to a bank or building society. The aim of the scheme is to encourage people to save by giving them tax benefits. The features of the scheme are:

- payments are deducted *after* the tax has been calculated; they show on the payslip
- the payments therefore do not feature on the P11 deduction sheet
- payments are made to a bank or building society by the employer
- interest on the investment is not taxed as long as the scheme is run for at least three years – *this* is the tax benefit (interest on investments is normally taxable)

GIVE AS YOU EARN (GAYE)

Give As You Earn (GAYE) is a government-instituted scheme operated by employers to encourage employees to give to charities. An employee may donate up to £1,200 of salary each year. The donation is deducted on each pay day by the employer from the employee's gross pay before the tax calculation is made. As far as the P11 is concerned:

- the 'pay for week or month' figure is entered in column 2 *after deduction* of the GAYE payment
- National Insurance contributions are unaffected – they are calculated on the pay before any GAYE deduction

The employer then normally pays the donations it has collected to the Charities Aid Foundation which then acts as a 'charity bank' in distributing funds to the charities nominated by the employee.

FURTHER ASPECTS OF PAY – HOLIDAY PAY

Holidays are normally covered in an employee's contract of employment. For example an employee may be granted four weeks paid holiday a year, plus bank holidays. For salaried staff, payment over the holiday period poses no problem – the monthly pay cheque or bank transfer is received as normal. There is no distinction between holiday pay and normal pay: holiday pay *is* normal pay.

Weekly paid workers, on the other hand, who are likely to be paid in cash on Fridays may well want holiday pay before they go away if they are taking a week or two off. This is, in effect, pay *in advance*.

The P11 deduction sheet is completed as follows:

- the pay for the holiday period is added up and entered on the P11 as if it were being paid on the last week of the holiday
- the Free Pay adjustment for that week will ensure that the correct amount of tax is paid
- the National Insurance contributions are entered on a week-by-week basis for each week of the holiday, added up for the holiday period and deducted from gross pay when the advance payment is made

PROFIT RELATED PAY (PRP)

Profit related pay (PRP) is an arrangement introduced by the government in 1987 whereby part of employees' pay is linked to the profit performance of the employing company in a particular accountng year and will be *tax free*, ie the employee will not have to pay tax on PRP.

Tax free profit related pay is calculated as 25% of earnings *before* PRP is added on, but limited to a certain maximum figure. This maximum is:

- £2,000 for accounting periods beginning in the 1998 calendar year
- £1,000 for accounting periods beginning in the 1999 calendar year

The normal formula for working out the maximum tax-free PRP for any given earnings figure is therefore:

Earnings x 0.25 (but not more than the maximum limit)

Any PRP paid in excess of the this will be taxed at normal rates. National Insurance contributions, however, must be paid on the total gross pay.

Set out below is an example of a calculation showing how the tax-free PRP is arrived at:

Tony Hague earns £20,000 a year. What is the tax free PRP he can be paid for an accounting year which started in January 1998?
The formula is:

Earnings x 0.25 (ie 25%), but not more than £2,000

Profit related pay = £20,000 x 0.25 = £5,000

But profit related pay cannot be more than £2,000

Therefore maximum profit related pay = £2,000

The government has announced that it will be phasing out the PRP scheme from the year 2000.

ADVANCES OF PAY

Employees are generally paid at the *end* of the week or month – ie when they have completed the appropriate hours and may also have earned commission, bonus payments and overtime which will be added to basic pay.

It is possible – although not very common – for an employee to be paid an *advance of pay* before the normal pay date. The word 'advance' here means 'loan' and this is basically what is involved. Take, for example, a new entrant to a company who will earn £1,250 *net* a month and will be paid at the end of the month – it is his or her first job and he or she will most likely be short of cash. The employer may advance some of the net salary – say £250 – to be paid to the employee at the beginning of the month to cover expenses. The payroll implications are as follows:

1   £250 of the net pay (£1,250) is given to the employee at the beginning of the month. This is noted by the employer but not entered on the P11.

2   The *full* gross pay is entered on the P11 at the end of the month and the tax and National Insurance calculated as appropriate.

3   The employee is paid the net pay figure worked out on the P11 *less the advance*. The advance therefore does not feature at all on the P11, but it is essential that it is deducted in the payroll process.

STATUTORY SICK PAY AND STATUTORY MATERNITY PAY

Although statutory sick pay and statutory maternity pay are not included in the NVQ Level 2 Accounting specifications, it is important to know about them if you are going to work with payroll. They are covered in outline here; further details may be found in Chapter 10.

The word 'statutory' means that something has to be done by law. Employers have a statutory duty to pay employees when they are off sick and when they are off work to have a baby. Many employers will pay their employees normal wages when they are off sick and many employers have their own maternity pay schemes. The statutory schemes are in place to ensure that sick or pregnant employees get a minimum rate of pay – employers *have* to pay them.

•   *Statutory Sick Pay (SSP)* is paid to most employees over the age of 16 who are away sick from work for four or more days (including weekends) in a row

•   *Statutory Maternity Pay (SMP)* is paid to female employees who are away from work to have a baby

Some of this money paid out by the employer *may* be reclaimed by deducting it from the National Insurance contributions due each month:

- *SSP* – only if the amount paid out exceeds a certain percentage of NICS

- *SMP* – most of the benefit paid can be reclaimed; smaller employers can reclaim all the money

statutory sick pay

Statutory Sick Pay (SSP) is payable to most employees

- aged 16 or over and under 65

- who are paid on average at least the NIC lower earnings limit

- who are away sick from work for four or more days in a row (including weekends) up to twenty-eight weeks

Employees are normally paid SSP *from the fourth day onwards*. SSP is not paid for the first three days of illness. It is a legal requirement that employers pay SSP where appropriate. Some employers may 'top up' this payment to provide the employee with full pay for the period of sickness, but here the employer stands the cost of the 'top up'. The object of the scheme is for the State to provide sick employees with a minimum income while they are incapacitated, whether it be because of serious illness or a bad curry.

SSP is calculated using tables issued by the Inland Revenue and is recorded on the P11 deductions working sheet.

SSP is recovered (where allowable) by deducting the amount paid from the monthly or quarterly payment of National Insurance to the Inland Revenue.

statutory maternity pay

Statutory Maternity Pay (SMP) is paid to an employee who is away from work to have a baby, even if she does not intend to return to work. It is payable for a period of up to 18 weeks (the Maternity Pay Period). SMP is payable by the employer and mostly recoverable by deduction from National Insurance contributions paid by the employer to the Inland Revenue.

SMP is payable:

- for the first six weeks at 90% of the employee's average weekly earnings

- for the remainder of Maternity Pay Period at the rates shown in the tables issued by the Inland Revenue

Unlike SSP, little of which may be reclaimed, most SMP is recoverable, plus an allowance for NIC paid on the SMP. It is recorded on the P11 deductions working sheet.

SMP is recovered (where allowable) by deducting the amount paid from the monthly or quarterly payment of National Insurance to the Inland Revenue.

CHAPTER SUMMARY

- There are two main types of state pension: the State Retirement Pension and the State Earnings Related Pension; contributions are made in the form of National Insurance contributions.

- Company pension schemes – occupational pensions – are operated by employers and financial services companies; contributions are generally made by employees and employers.

- Employees may 'top up' company schemes by making Additional Voluntary Contributions (AVCs) through the employer or Free Standing Additional Voluntary Contributions (FSAVCs) through a financial services company.

- Private pension plans – available to the employed and self-employed – are arrangements between individuals and financial services companies; they are fully portable.

- Care must be taken when completing an employee's P11 deduction sheet that the pension deductions are only made when appropriate and at the correct stage of the calculations.

- Employees may make savings payments through the payroll – the scheme is known as Save As You Earn (SAYE).

- Employees may give to charities through the payroll – the scheme is known as Give As You Earn (GAYE).

- Holiday pay most commonly affects weekly paid employees who may be paid holiday pay in advance; monthly paid employees are normally paid in line with the usual payroll arrangements when they are away.

- Profit related pay (PRP) is a scheme whereby an employee may receive a tax-free proportion of pay which is directly related to the amount of profit the employer makes.

- Advances of pay are loans of net pay made to employees needing cash before a salary payment is due.

- Statutory Sick Pay (SSP) is the rate of pay employers by law are obliged to pay to employees who are off sick. Some SSP may be recovered by deducting it from National Insurance payments made to the Inland Revenue.

- Statutory Maternity Pay (SMP) is the rate of pay employers by law are obliged to pay to employees who are off work to give birth. Most SMP may be recovered by deducting it from National Insurance payments made to the Inland Revenue.

KEY TERMS

state retirement pension	the basic state pension, received by those who have made National Insurance contributioms; payable to men at 65 and women at 60
SERPS	the State Earnings Related Pension Scheme (SERPS) is based on earnings made during an employee's working life, provided that not contracted-out NI contributions have been made
company schemes	pension schemes, organised by the employer and contributed to by the employer and, in many cases, the employee too
defined benefit scheme	a company scheme where the final pension is calculated on the basis of the number of years worked and the final salary
money purchase scheme	a scheme where the contributions are paid into a fund managed by a financial services company
Additional Voluntary Contribution	AVCs are extra pension contributions made by employees through a company scheme to bring the level of contribution up the maximum allowable for tax relief, eg up to 15% of pay
FSAVCs	Free Standing Additional Voluntary Contributions (FSAVCs) are AVCs that are made independently by the employee through a financial services company rather than through a company scheme.
private pension plan	a private pension plan may be set up by a financial services company on behalf of an employee or a self-employed person, who is allowed to invest between 17.5% and 40% of earnings tax free
Save As You Earn (SAYE)	a savings scheme operated by employers which enables employees to save with banks and building societies for three years or more and receive interest tax-free
Give As You Earn (GAYE)	a scheme whereby employers can deduct up to £1,200 of salary annually tax free and donate the funds to charities of the employee's choice through the Charities Aid Foundation
holiday pay	wages paid in advance of time taken off

	for holidays, normally to weekly paid employees
profit related pay	tax free amounts paid to employees, linked to the level of profits made by the employer
advances of pay	loans of net pay made to employees in advance of the wages/salary payment date

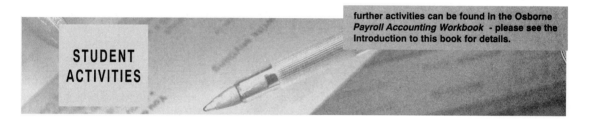

STUDENT ACTIVITIES

further activities can be found in the Osborne *Payroll Accounting Workbook* - please see the Introduction to this book for details.

5.1 Every retired person in the UK is entitled to receive the basic state retirement pension.

True or false?

State the reasons for your answer.

5.2 SERPS is available to employees who have paid

(a) not contracted-out National Insurance contributions

(b) contracted-out National Insurance contributions

(c) contributions to an approved company pension scheme

(d) additional voluntary contributions (AVCs)

Choose *one* option from the above.

5.3 Explain the difference between

(a) a defined benefit scheme

(b) defined contribution scheme

5.4 Explain the difference between

(a) AVCs

(b) FSAVCs

Which of the two would be dealt with on a regular basis by a payroll clerk?

5.5 State two advantages to an employee of taking out a private pension plan.

5.6   What difference will it make to a payroll clerk working out income tax if an employee

(a)   pays contributions into an approved company pension scheme

(b)   pays contributions into an approved private pension scheme

(c)   pays FSAVCs

(d)   wants to benefit from SERPS

5.7   Melissa earns £1,000 gross monthly (assume that there is no overtime, commission or any extra payments). Melissa has arranged with the Charities Aid Foundation to give £600 a year to charity through GAYE by equal monthly instalments. What is the figure

(a)   looked up as 'earnings' in the National Insurance tables?

(b)   entered each month on the P11 in column 2 as monthly pay for income tax purposes?

5.8   What is the maximum amount of tax-free profit related pay the following employees will be entitled to under current regulations? In each case the accounting periods start in 1998.

employee	annual earnings (before PRP)
Jim	£3,000
Bob	£3,500
Asif	£8,000
Hans	£10,000
Mel	£12,000
Yousef	£15,000

5.9*   An employer can recover all statutory sick pay paid to employees by deducting it from the National Insurance contributions made to the Inland Revenue.

True or false?

5.10*   For what period and at what rates is Statutory Maternity Pay payable?

* optional questions – the subjects are not included in the NVQ Accounting specifications.

6 LEAVING AND STARTING EMPLOYMENT

this chapter covers . . .

The chapters so far in this book have covered the procedures for calculating pay and deductions for existing employees. In this chapter we turn to the procedures involved when

- an employee leaves a place of employment
- an employee starts a new job

These situations are explained in this order because the main document we will be dealing with – the P45 – is completed by the employer for an employee leaving a job and is taken to the new place of employment by the employee.

We will also explain what happens when an employee starts a job for the first time – obviously with no P45 – and signs a P46 form.

NVQ PERFORMANCE CRITERIA COVERED

unit 3: RECORDING PAYROLL TRANSACTIONS

element 1

operate and maintain a payroll accounting system

- ❏ the current payroll status of employees is accurately recorded
- ❏ statutory and non-statutory deductions are correctly calculated and made in accordance with legal and organisational requirements
- ❏ the organisation's procedures and timescales are observed

EMPLOYEES LEAVING

Employees leave for a variety of reasons: they get another job, they retire, they are made redundant, or they may even be sacked, or die. When an employee leaves a job it is essential that the department or person dealing with payroll makes sure that:

- the employee receives the right amount of pay up to the last day of working – including any arrears and holiday pay

- the date of leaving is noted in the box on the P11 deductions sheet

- the Inland Revenue is notified with details of pay and tax in the current tax year – on the front sheet of a form P45

- the employee is given the remaining sheets of the P45 (unless, of course, the employee has died)

FORM P45

A form P45 is a four part form issued by the Inland Revenue and completed by an employer when an employee

- leaves for another job

- leaves and has no job to go to

- retires or dies

The appropriate parts of the P45 will then be handed by the employee to any new employer. The distribution of the four parts of the P45 is illustrated below and explained on the following pages.

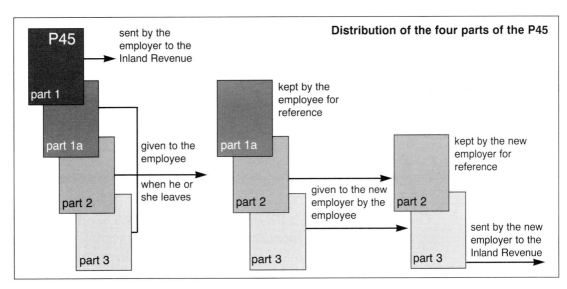

COMPLETING THE P45

As we have seen, the P45 is a form in four parts. It is illustrated on the opposite page. The employer (whom the employee is leaving) completes the top half of the P45, in biro and block capitals – these details will imprint through on all the copies below. The information is set out in numbered boxes. Relevant details include:

box 1	the PAYE reference of the employer – a unique reference code issued by the Inland Revenue and used in all communications between the employer and the tax office
box 2	the employee's National Insurance number (this will be on the P11 and in the payroll records)
box 3	the name of the employee
box 4	the leaving date
box 5	the most up-to-date tax code (as shown on the P11)
box 6	the total pay and tax to date for the current tax year (from the P11) – including any previous jobs in the current tax year
box 7	pay and tax, but only if paid on week1/month 1 basis

The remaining information includes the employee's works details, address and a signed declaration by the employer that the details are correct.

Part 1 of the P45 is sent by the employer to the Inland Revenue, Parts 1a, 2 and 3 are given to the employee who is leaving.

If the employee gets a new job, he or she gives Parts 2 and 3 to the new employer, who in turn completes and sends Part 3 to the tax office.

importance of the P45

The P45 is a vital document which

- tells the tax office the pay and tax details of an employee who moves job (Part 1)
- provides the employee with the pay and tax details of the job he or she has just left (Part 1a)
- tells any new employer the pay and tax details that will be needed for the new P11 deductions sheet (Part 2)
- tells the tax office when the employee gets a new job (Part 3)

	Details of employee leaving work	**P45**
Inland **Revenue** ·	Copy for Tax Office	**Part 1**

District number   Reference number

1 PAYE Reference   *107*   *H23*

2 Employee's National Insurance number   *AB 17 49 06 A*
(Mr Mrs Miss Ms)

3 Surname
(in capitals)   *HENDERSON*   *MRS*

First name(s)
(in capitals)   *EDWINA*

Day   Month   Year

4 Leaving date (in figures)   *29   01   1999*

5 Tax Code at leaving date. *If Week 1 or Month 1 basis
applies, write 'X' in the box marked* Week 1 or Month 1

Code   Week 1 or Month 1

404L

6 Last entries on
*Deductions
Working Sheet* (P11)
**Complete only if
Tax Code is cumulative.**
Make no entry here if
Week 1 or Month 1 basis
applies. Go to item 7.

Week or
month number   Week   Month   *10*

Total pay to date   £ *12570 50* p

Total tax to date   £ *2007 57* p

7 This employment pay
and tax. ■ *No entry
needed if Tax Code is
cumulative and amounts
are same as item 6 entry.*

Total pay
in this employment   £   p

Total tax
in this employment   £   p

8 Works number/
Payroll number   *916*

9 Department or
branch if any   *—*

10 Employee's
private
address and
Postcode

*79 BLENHEIM CRESCENT
STOURMINSTER
ST3 1XJ*

11 I certify that the details entered above in items 1 to 9 are correct

Employer's
name,
address and
Postcode

*MOORFIELD EMPLOYMENT AGENCY
17 PALACE COURT
STOURMINSTER ST1 0RY*

Date   *29 / 01 / 1999*

For Tax Office use

To the employer

- Complete this form following the 'Employee leaving' instructions in the *Employer's
  Quick Guide to PAYE and NICs* (cards CWG1). Make sure the details are clear on all
  four parts of this form. Make sure your name and address is shown on Parts 1 and 1A.

- Detach Part 1 and send it to your Tax Office immediately.

- Hand Parts 1A, 2 and 3 (unseparated) to your employee when
  he or she leaves.

- If the employee has died, write 'D' in this box and send all four
  parts of this form (unseparated) to your Tax Office immediately.

P45

SPECIMEN

P45: Part 1 completed by the employer

QUERIES WITH P45s

There are a number of situations where completing a P45 is not straightforward and where queries are likely to arise.

lost or incorrect P45s

If an employee contacts you and tells you that the P45 is lost or if you find that there is a mistake on an issued P45, the employee should contact the tax office. Under *no* circumstances should a P45 be amended or reissued.

paying an employee after issuing a P45

If you find that a further payment is due to an employee after a P45 has been issued – eg a bonus payment, commission due to an employee who has left – the money should be paid after deduction of basic rate tax (not lower rate). The P11 is completed in the appropriate week/month, the code amended to BR and tax deducted at the basic rate – no pay adjustment is made.

ex-employees and state benefit

Employees who leave and wish to claim benefit (such as unemployment benefit) should present Parts 2 and 3 of the P45 at the DSS office; this should enable them eventually to receive a tax refund.

death of an employee

On the death of the employee, a P45 should be completed in the normal way, but instead of giving Part 1a to 3 to the employee, the employer should write 'D' in the box at the bottom of Part 1 and send the four parts to the tax office.

National Insurance

Note that the P45 only covers the deduction of *income tax*.

STARTING EMPLOYMENT

The P45, as we have seen, forms a vital link between employments. It makes sure that the tax office is kept up-to-date with details of earnings and tax paid; it prevents people fiddling the amount of tax they have to pay – for example by understating their earnings when they change jobs.

When an employee starts work with a new employer the payroll clerk will have therefore have a certain amount of paperwork to deal with, including the P45.

payroll records

The person dealing with a new employee's payroll arrangements should first of all ensure that there is a payroll record for the employee. This may be a paper-based file, or it may be a record on a computer database. It will normally contain:

- personal details such as the name and address of the employee
- works details – department, employee reference number (to be used in payroll transactions)
- rates of pay
- date of joining the organisation
- banking details (bank sort code and account number) if payment of wages or salary is to be made direct to a bank

The person dealing with payroll will normally get these details from the Human Resources Department (which will have drawn up the contract of employment); if the business is small, the details will come from the boss. If the business is very small (eg a sole trader) the same person is likely to deal with everything – from drawing up the contract to working out the wages and signing the wages cheques.

P45 or no P45?

The first question facing the person dealing with a new employee's payroll arrangements is – has the new employee got a P45? If there is a P45, matters are relatively straightforward; if the employee does not have a P45, there are a number of different procedures that can be adopted, depending on the circumstances. We will deal with these on pages 81 to 84. First, however, we will look at the procedures to be adopted when a new employee has a P45.

A NEW EMPLOYEE WITH A P45

The employee should give the employer Parts 2 and 3 of the P45 which will show details of the previous employment. If by any chance the employee hands over Part 1a, this should be given back – it is the employee's reference copy! The steps that the employer should then take are as follows:

P45 Part 3

Part 3 should be completed and sent to the Inland Revenue without delay. The employer will complete the details from item 7 onwards. The form is illustrated on the next page. The details are explained on page 79.

SPECIMEN

Inland Revenue

New employee details | **P45**
For completion by new employer | Part 3

District number | Reference number

1 Previous PAYE Reference   107   /   H23

2 Employee's National Insurance number   AB 17 79 06 A
(Mr Mrs Miss Ms)

3 Surname   HENDERSON   MRS

First name(s)   EDWINA

	Day	Month	Year
4 Date left previous employment	29	01	1999

5 Tax Code at leaving date. 'X' in the box means Week 1 or Month 1 basis applies
Code   404L   Week 1 or Month 1

6 Last entries on Deductions Working Sheet (P11) If there is an 'X' at item 5, there will be no entries here

Week or month number | Week | Month: 10

Total pay to date £ 12570, 50 p

Total tax to date £ 2007, 57 p

To the new employer
Complete items 7 to 16 below and send this page of the form only to your Tax Office immediately.

7 New PAYE Reference   107 / R24

	Day	Month	Year
8 Date employment started (in figures)	02	02	1999

9 Tick here if you want these details to be shown on tax code notifications   ✓

Works/Payroll number   1026
Department or branch if any   —

10 Enter P if employee will not be paid by you between date employment began and next 5 April

11 Enter code in use if different to code at item 5

12 If tax at item 6 above is not the same as tax entered on *Deductions Working Sheet* **(P11) from the Tax Tables, write the Tax Tables figure here** £

13 Employee's private address   79 BLENHEIM CRESCENT
STOURMINSTER   Postcode ST3 1XJ

	Day	Month	Year		
14 Employee's date of birth (if known)	19	04	1976	**15 Employee's job title or description**	CLERICAL ASSISTANT

16 Declaration. I have prepared a *Deductions Working Sheet* (P11) in accordance with the details above.

Employer   OSBORNE ELECTRONICS LIMITED

Address   UNIT 12 ELWOOD ESTATE

P45   STOURMINSTER   Postcode ST1 4LJ   Date 2/2/99

P45: Part 3 completed by the new employer, ready for sending off to the local Inland Revenue office

box 7 the PAYE reference of the new employer – which should be well known to the payroll staff

box 8 the date employment started – accuracy is important here for tax period purposes – see the employee's payroll record

box 9 the payroll reference number given by the employer – this is also written on the P11 deductions sheet

Box 10 a 'P' is inserted here if the employee starts work in one tax year and is first paid in the next, eg starts work on 1 April and is paid on 30 April

Box 11 if the tax code has changed since the last employment – eg if the new employment starts in a different tax year when the code is likely to have increased – the new code is entered here

Box 12 the new employer must check that the tax previously deducted (see box 6) is correct for the stated amount of taxable pay (see box 6) – if it is not, the correct amount is entered here (and on the P11) and the matter will be sorted out between the employee and the Inland Revenue tax office, *not by the new employer*

Box 13 the employee's private address – see the employee's payroll record

Box 14 the employee's date of birth – see the employee's payroll record

Box 15 the employee's job title or description – see the employee's payroll record

Box 16 the Declaration is not signed by the employer – just the name and address are inserted

P45 Part 2

Part 2 of the P45 is the employer's reference copy. It should be retained by the employer for at least three years after the end of the tax year to which it refers. Remember that Part 3 should be sent to the tax office as soon as it and the P11 (see next page) have been completed.

P11		Name: *E Henderson*					
Month no	Week no	Pay in the week or month 2	Total pay to date 3	Total Free Pay to date 4a	Total taxable pay to date (Column 3 minus 4a) 5	Total tax due to date 6	Tax deducted or refunded in the week or month 7
	41						
	42						
10	43		12,570.50	3374.20	9196.30	2007.57	
	43						
	43						
	43						
11	43	1,500	14,070.50	3711.62	10358.88	2264.08	256.51

total pay and tax from previous employment entered on P11 from P45

pay for the first month from new employment

P11 deductions working sheet

A P11 deductions working sheet should be completed for each new employee. The procedure is as follows:

- Enter the pay details from box 6 on the P45 on the appropriate line on the P11 (here month 10) – this applies to *cumulative codes only*.* Calculate the tax due on this amount of pay by using the tax tables and completing the boxes for free pay, taxable pay and tax due to date.

- Check your tax calculation with the tax figure in box 6 of the P45.

- If there is a difference, check your workings and if there is still a difference, enter your figure in box 12 of the P45 Part 3 – this will tell the tax office that there is an error which they should take up with the employee.

- On the first pay day in the new employment complete the appropriate line on the P11, picking up the figures from the previous employment which appear above the entry for the first pay day.

*Note that if the employee has been on a Week1/Month1 basis in the previous employment there will be no figures for pay and tax on the new employer's copy of the P45; the new employer will have to wait for a P6 advising the figures and work on a Week1/Month1 basis in the meantime.

NEW EMPLOYEES WITHOUT A P45

If an employee – full-time, part-time or casual – starts work with an employer and does not have (or cannot get hold of) a P45, there are a number of different courses of action to take, depending on the circumstances.

will the employee work for one week or less?

Take the following courses of action:

circumstance	action
when the employee has another job and will earn more than the PAYE threshold	*complete a P11 and deduct tax using the BR (basic rate) code and NICS as appropriate*
when the employee does not have another job and will earn more than the PAYE threshold	*complete a P11 and deduct tax using the emergency code on a week 1 basis (and any NICS)*
when total pay is less than the PAYE threshold, but equal to, or more than the NIC lower earnings limit	*complete a P11, recording 'NI' in the code box and NICS in the appropriate columns*
when total pay in the week is less than the NIC lower earnings limit	*you do not need to complete a P11, but you must keep normal payroll records: ie name, address and amount of pay of employee*

employee who works for more than one week – P46

If an employee is going to work for more than one week, a P46 must be completed. Remember that this applies to full-time, part-time or casual employees.

The function of a P46 is to tell the tax office about

- employees who do not have a P45 – eg school leavers
- employees who have previously been paid below the PAYE threshold (see above)

Now look at the P46 illustrated on page 83 and read the notes on the opposite page. The printed P46 is in two parts, the second part being a carbon copy.

completing the P46 – employee

The employer should give the P46 to the employee and ask him or her to read Statements A, B and C (top left of form) and tick and sign where appropriate:

Statement A applies to employees who are starting their first regular job since leaving full-time education, and who have received no benefit

Statement B applies to employees who are starting the job as their only or main job

Statement C applies to employees who receive a pension as well as income from the job

The employee should then complete the bottom of the form as appropriate, listing, with appropriate *dates,* for the last *twelve month* period:

* any employment
* any periods of self-employment
* any benefit received
* any periods spent not working
* the employee's National Insurance number

The section 'Additional information' should include

* the name and address of any employers
* the business name and address if self-employed
* the type of any benefit received
* details of any non-working periods – eg 'full-time education'

completing the P46 – employer

When the employee has filled in his or her sections as appropriate, the employer completes the form and sends it off to the tax office so that the Inland Revenue can issue a tax code for the employee.

This sounds fairly straightforward, but it is not quite as simple as it seems, because decisions have to be made about what type of temporary tax code should be used in the meantime – this is to be noted on the P46 in the section 'Coding Information.' What are the possibilities?

circumstance	action
the employee has not ticked any statement and has not signed the form – for example someone who is starting a second job	*complete a P11 and deduct tax using the BR (basic rate) code; send the P46 to the tax office*

SPECIMEN

Inland Revenue

PAYE Employer's notice to Tax Office **P46**

Use this form to tell the Tax Office about
- employees who do not have a form P45 or
- employees previously paid below the PAYE threshold.

To be completed by the employee

Read each statement below carefully. Tick **each one** that applies to you. If none of them apply, do not sign the statement. Complete the lower part of the form.

Statement A   ✓

This is my first regular job since leaving full-time education. I have not claimed Jobseekers Allowance, or income support paid because of unemployment since then. ☐

Statement B   ☑

This is my only or main job.

Statement C

I receive a pension as well as the income from this job. ☐

I confirm I have ticked the statements that apply to me.

Signed _C Compton_ Date _5 May 99_

To be completed by the employer

Employer's name

OSBORNE ELECTRONICS UNITED

Employer's address

UNIT 12 ELWOOD ESTATE

STOURMINSTER

Postcode _ST1 4LJ_

	District no.	Reference
Employer's PAYE reference	1 0 7	R24

	Day	Month	Year
Date this form was completed	06	05	1999

Your Employer's Quick Guide to PAYE and NICs (CWG1) tells you how to complete this form and what to do with it – see Card 8.

P46(1997)   BMSD1/97

Employee's details – *to be entered by employer*

	Letters	Numbers	Numbers	Numbers	Letter
National Insurance number	A8	20	01	51	A

Surname including title Mr/Mrs/Miss/Ms

Title	Surname
MR	COMPTON

First name(s)

ALEXANDER

Home address

25 ACACIA AVENUE

STOURMINSTER

Postcode _ST5 0BE_

Date of birth (in figures)	Day	Month	Year
	09	07	1950

Put 'M' for male or 'F' for female in box _M_

Works or payroll number, *if any* _1073_

Branch or department, *if any*

Job title

DRIVER

Date employment started	Day	Month	Year
	05	05	1999

Coding information *to be completed by employer*

Existing employee now above PAYE threshold ☐
enter X in box if this applies

New employee who has signed statement *enter letter here* _B_

New employee who has not signed a statement ☐

Code operated for this employee _450L_

Enter X in box if code operated on week1/month 1 basis _X_

Employee *If you wish you can detach this part and send it to the Tax Office yourself. Ask your employer for the Tax Office's address.*

Your employer's PAYE reference _____

Completing this form will help your employer and the Tax Office to give you a correct PAYE code. Without it you may pay too much or too little tax.
Please list below in date order all the jobs you have had and any periods when you were out of work during the last **twelve months**. Please do not leave any gaps between the periods. If you were claiming benefit while you were out of work please show this in the space provided.

	Your National Insurance number	Letters	Numbers	Numbers	Numbers	Letter

Under **Additional information** give the following details
- your employer's name and address if you were employed
- your business name and address if you were self-employed
- the type of benefit you claimed while out of work
- what you were doing if you were not working and not claiming benefit, for example, in full time education.
Use a separate sheet if there is not enough space on this slip.

Dates		*Tick one box for each period*				
From	To	Employed	Self employed	Claiming benefit	Not working	Additional information
		☐	☐	☐	☐	
		☐	☐	☐	☐	
		☐	☐	☐	☐	

P46

P46 completed by a new employee and the employer

circumstance	action
the employee has signed the form and ticked statement A only, or statements A and B – this is normally the case with a school or college leaver	*complete a P11 and deduct tax using the emergency code on a cumulative basis, but make sure any previous earnings for the tax year are entered on the P11; send the P46 to the tax office*
the employee has signed the form and ticked statement B only – this is often the case for someone who has had a part-time job but is now working full-time and is earning more than the PAYE threshold	*complete a P11 and deduct tax using the emergency code on a week 1/month 1 basis; make sure any previous earnings for the tax year are entered on the P11; send the P46 to the tax office*
the employee has signed the form and ticked statement C only, or statements B and C	*complete a P11 and deduct tax using the BR (basic rate) code; send the P46 to the tax office*

employees earning below the PAYE threshold

All the cases above relate to employees earning above the *PAYE threshold* – ie the weekly or monthly amount (set out in the tax tables) above which income tax becomes payable. Most employees will earn amounts above the threshold, but occasionally you will encounter people earning lower amounts – eg permanent part-timers. You treat these employees in much the same way as you treat temporary staff who do not need a P46:

circumstance	action
when total pay is less than the PAYE threshold, but equal to, or more than the NIC lower earnings limit	*complete a P11, recording 'NI' in the code box and NICS in the appropriate columns; keep the P46 for reference*
when total pay in the week is less than the NIC lower earnings limit	*you do not need to complete a P11, but you must keep normal payroll records: ie name, address and amount of pay of employee; keep the P46 for reference*

CASE STUDY

NEW ENTRANTS – PAYROLL QUERIES

You work in the payroll section of Tropic Manufacturing Ltd which makes ice cream products. Following a hot spell in July a number of new operatives have been recruited for the production line. Some have P45s, some do not. You have to sort out the documentation for the following:

Lollyta	has a P45 but the amount of tax paid shown on the form does not tie up with the amount of taxable pay shown
Rashid	has signed up for four days only – he will earn less than the PAYE threshold and the NIC lower earnings limit; he has no P45
Neeta	has also signed up for four days only – she will earn less than the PAYE threshold but more than the NIC lower earnings limit; she has no P45
Cath	is a school leaver – she has no P45 and has not claimed benefit; she will work full-time for two months for Tropic Manufacturing and will earn a wage over the PAYE threshold; there is no pension arrangement
Craig	has worked for Tropic Manufacturing Ltd on a part-time basis, below the PAYE threshold; he is now going to work full-time for two months and earn a wage over the PAYE threshold

solution

Lollyta	you should complete a P11 deductions working sheet showing the pay and tax deducted from the previous employment; when this calculation is checked using the tax tables, the discrepancy will appear; it must be sorted out between Lollyta and the tax office; you should enter the correct amount of tax to be deducted in box 12 of Part 3 of the P45 (which will be sent to the tax office) and also on the P11 – you should *not* attempt to correct the error
Rashid	*no* P11 is needed – you should record the name and address of the employee and the pay for the four days; no P46 is needed
Neeta	a P11 is needed – you should enter 'NI' in the tax code box and complete the NIC columns as normal; no P46 is needed
Cath	a P46 should be completed by Cath and the employer; Cath should tick statements A and B and sign and date the form; she should also complete the bottom of the form with details of the last 12 months' activities; the employer will complete the form and send it to the tax office; the emergency code will be applied on a cumulative basis until a tax code is issued by the tax office
Craig	a P46 should be completed by Craig and the employer; Craig should tick statement B and sign and date the form; he should also complete the bottom of the form with details of the last 12 months' work (the earnings are entered on the P11); the employer will complete the form and send it to the tax office; the emergency code will be applied on a week 1/month 1 basis until a tax code is issued by the tax office

CHAPTER

SUMMARY

- When an employee leaves for any reason (eg resignation, retirement, redundancy, dismissal, death) the employer issues a P45 – a four-part Inland Revenue form.

- The P45 records pay and tax deductions for the tax year in which it is issued.

- The P45 is important because it provides PAYE details for the employer, the employee, any new employer and the tax office.

- The P45 will be needed by the Department of Social Security if the employee needs to claim unemployment benefit after leaving a job.

- Once a P45 has been issued it cannot under any circumstances be amended by the employer – any queries have to be taken up with the tax office.

- When an employee starts a new job the employer must first find out if the employee has a P45.

- If the new employee has a P45, Parts 2 and 3 should be handed to the employer for completion; Part 3 is then sent to the tax office.

- If the employee has no P45 (eg a school leaver) a P46 will need to be completed by the employer and employee, *unless* the work undertaken is for less than a week.

- An employer taking on a new employee should ensure that

  – there is a payroll record set up for the employee

  – a P11 deductions working sheet is completed for the employee (unless the employee is temporary and earns less than the PAYE threshold and NIC lower earnings limit)

KEY

TERMS

P45	an Inland Revenue form in four parts:
	Part 1 – sent by the employer to the tax office
	Part 1a – kept by the employee
	Part 2 – kept by the new employer
	Part 3 – sent by the new employer to the tax office
payroll record	A file kept by the employer containing details of the employee's name, address, works and wages or salary payment details
PAYE threshold	the amount of pay above which income tax becomes payable
NIC lower earnings limit	the amount of earnings over which National Insurance contributions become payable
P46	an Inland Revenue form completed by an employer and employee when the employee has no P45
P11	the P11 deductions working sheet is an Inland Revenue form on which pay, tax and National Insurance contributions are entered

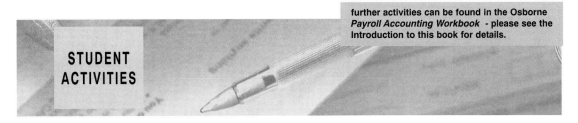

further activities can be found in the Osborne *Payroll Accounting Workbook* - please see the Introduction to this book for details.

STUDENT ACTIVITIES

6.1 (a) Under what circumstances is a P45 issued?

(b) What happens to the four parts of a P45?

6.2 (a) Under what circumstances is a P46 issued?

(b) What happens to the completed P46?

6.3 You are working in a payroll office. It is 2 April. What would you do in the following situations? Mention any forms and documentation that you might use.

(a) Anita left your employment a month ago. She telephones to say that her accountant has found an error on the P45 which you issued – apparently the total of tax deducted during the tax year was incorrect.

(b) Chris left your employment a month ago. You issued a P45 at the time but now find that he is due a productivity bonus of £250.

(c) Robin, one of your drivers, has a heart attack and dies while still in your employment. Someone tells you that you do not need to issue a P45 because Robin will not be getting another job.

(d) Paul has just started work for you. He forgot his P45 on the first day but has now remembered and has passed the form to your office in an envelope. When you open the envelope you find that it has Parts 1a, 2 and 3 in it.

(e) Tim, who has started work at the beginning of April, will not be paid until the end of the month. He asks if this will cause a problem with his P45 – he points out that it is for the tax year which will end on 5 April.

6.4 You are working in the payroll office. It is now 5 May. What would you do in the following situations? Mention any forms and documentation that you might use.

(a) Tanya, who has started work at the beginning of May, has handed you her P45. You set up a new P11 for her and check the pay and tax to date totals. You find that there is an error on the P45: Tanya has paid too much tax.

(b) Dave has been working part-time for your organisation, but has now secured a full-time permanent post with you. As he has only been working a few hours a week and has earned less than the PAYE threshold and NIC lower earnings limit, you have not been completing a P11 for him. He says "I guess I will have to pay tax and National Insurance now, but I hope you won't have to take account of all my part-time earnings over the last few months – I don't want to be taxed on them too!"

(c) Jo has been taken on for four days in a busy time. She will earn less than the PAYE threshold but more than the NIC lower earnings limit.

(d) Dan is a school leaver who has been doing unpaid voluntary work since last summer. He has been taken on for twelve months as a trainee sales manager. He has no P45 as he has no employment history and has not claimed benefit.

7 PAYING EMPLOYEES

this chapter covers . . .

The chapters so far in this book have covered the procdures for calculating pay and deductions for employees. In this chapter we turn to the payment of wages and salaries and the maintenance of payment records. The chapter covers:

- the payslip – how to read one
- paying by cash – the cash analysis and withdrawal of cash from the bank
- paying by cheque – preparing cheques and obtaining authorisation
- paying by credit transfer – preparing the summary
- paying by electronic transfer through the banking system (BACS)
- dealing with problems and queries

NVQ PERFORMANCE CRITERIA COVERED

unit 3: RECORDING PAYROLL TRANSACTIONS

element 2

make authorised payments to employees

- ❑ payslip advice records are correctly prepared and reconciled with cash records
- ❑ due payments are correctly processed within specified deadlines
- ❑ payroll information is clearly explained to employees and enquiries from employees are handled courteously and confidentially
- ❑ annual tax records and other relevant documentation is made available to employees promptly
- ❑ defined procedures for dealing with unclaimed pay are strictly followed
- ❑ safety and security procedures for the handling of cash and cheques are always followed
- ❑ confidentiality and security of information is maintained
- ❑ discrepancies, unusual features or queries are identified and referred to the appropriate person or resolved
- ❑ documentation is correctly filed

THE PAYSLIP

Employees must by law be given a *payslip* showing gross pay and the deductions made to arrive at net pay. There is no set format for a payslip. Some organisations will write or type out the details on a printed form, other organisations may use a computer payroll program which will calculate all the figures and automatically print out the payslip. A typical payslip is shown below.

OSBORNE ELECTRONICS LTD		Pay Advice	Week 2
payments		**deductions**	
	£		£
Basic pay	180.00	Income tax	51.11
Overtime	80.00	National Insurance	25.45
Bonus	60.00	Superannuation	9.00
TOTAL GROSS PAY	320.00	SAYE	00.00
		TOTAL DEDUCTIONS	85.56
Gross pay to date	620.00		
Taxable pay to date	446.26	TOTAL NET PAY	234.44
Date	**Employee**	Income tax to date	97.61
16.04.99	J Smithers	National Insurance to date	48.90

details on the payslip

As noted above, there is no set format for a payslip. The details that will normally be found are:

essential details	optional details
employer name	tax code
employee name	payroll number
gross pay	National Insurance number
statutory sick pay	method of payment
statutory maternity pay	
period (week/month)	
deductions made, eg	
- tax for the period	
- tax and NI to date	
- NI for the period	
- employee's pension payment	
net pay	

payroll checking and authorisation

Clearly the 'garbage in, garbage out' principle will operate here – the payslip will only be accurate as long as the information provided is correct, for example:

- the amount of gross pay – including any overtime, commission, or bonus
- the tax code
- the employee's identity (it has not been unknown for the right pay to go to the wrong person!)

It is essential therefore that all these payroll details are

1   checked

2   authorised before processing

scheduling to deadlines

Weekly pay is normally paid on a Friday and monthly pay at or towards the end of the month. It is essential that timescales are observed for making sure that employees are paid promptly and provided with a payslip at the same time. The larger the organisation, very often the longer the lead time, particularly if the system is computerised. You may therefore sometimes find a delay in the payment of overtime – extra hours worked in January may be paid in February – especially as overtime hours have to be approved and authorised before payment can be made.

providing information to employees

Employees may query payslips if they are not happy with them. For example you may be asked:

"Please check my overtime; I am sure I did more hours than that."

"What has happened to my pay rise?"

"Why has my tax code changed?– I have had to pay more tax."

You will see from this that many of the queries will have to be referred elsewhere – to the Human Resources Department in the case of a larger organisation or to the boss in the case of a small business. Some queries you may be able to deal with yourself, for example the increase in the tax code after the start of the new tax year, brought about by the standard budget changes in personal allowances.

In Chapter 8 we will deal with the annual return of payroll information to the Inland Revenue on form P35; at the same time each year each employee will be given a P60 setting out the pay and deductions for the year. You will need to be familiar with the P60 and be able to explain it to new employees.

RECORDING PAYROLL INFORMATION

who needs the information?

You will appreciate from the previous page that payroll records have to be *accurate* because pay is an important part of the contract between employer and employee. The employee must be paid the right amount! There are additional reasons why the information has to be accurate:

- payroll details have to be entered into the financial accounting system of the business to provide data for the profit statement (see Chapter 9)

- payroll details help a business *cost* its operations – they will make possible, for example, the calculation of the labour cost of a particular department, or the labour cost of a particular operation

- payroll details have to be provided to the Inland Revenue: for example tax and National Insurance PAYE contributions sent off monthly and summarised annually – incorrect figures could land the organisation with an Inland Revenue inspection or penalties

information sources – payroll analysis sheet

The forms and documents we have seen so far do not *individually* provide a complete picture of all the information needed by a payroll department:

- the P11 deductions working sheet enables the deductions to be calculated, but it does not show the employee's net pay, nor the employer's National Insurance contribution

- the payslip does not show the employer's NIC or pension contributions

- the employee's payroll record will only show static personal details

Many organisations therefore use a sheet known as a *payroll analysis* to *bring all this information together.* An example is shown on the next page.

The payroll analysis shows the figures for each 'run' of the payroll, ie each week or month that the calculations and payments are made. The details include:

- employee name and payroll reference

- the make up of gross pay – basic pay plus overtime, bonus etc

- PAYE deductions – tax and National Insurance (employer and employee)

- other deductions, eg pensions, including the employer's contributions

Another function of the payroll analysis is that it will *reconcile* the individual amounts that make up the payroll with the totals for the period. The payroll analysis sheet acts as a cross-checking device (see page 93).

OSBORNE ELECTRONICS payroll analysis sheet tax year ..../......... week/month..........

employee reference	employee name	Earnings				Deductions				Employer's National Insurance Contributions £	Employer's Pension Contributions £	Net Pay £
		Basic £	Overtime £	Bonus £	Total Gross Pay £	Income Tax £	National Insurance £	Pension Contributions £	Total Deductions £			
2345	W Rowberry	205.00	25.00	15.00	245.00	35.00	19.50	10.25	64.75	24.50	10.25	180.25
2346	M Richardson	205.00	10.00	15.00	230.00	32.50	18.00	10.25	60.75	23.05	10.25	169.25
2347	D Stanbury	205.00	25.00	15.00	245.00	35.00	19.50	-	54.50	24.50	-	190.50
2348	D Payne	205.00	25.00	15.00	245.00	35.00	19.50	-	54.50	24.50	-	190.50
2349	K Peters	205.00	10.00	15.00	230.00	32.50	18.00	10.25	60.75	23.05	10.25	169.25
2350	O Robinson	205.00	25.00	15.00	245.00	35.00	19.50	10.25	64.75	24.50	10.25	180.25
TOTALS		1230.00	120.00	90.00	1440.00	205.00	114.00	41.00	360.00	144.10	41.00	1080.00

a payroll analysis sheet (for weekly payroll)

cross-checking the payroll analysis sheet

The payroll analysis sheet on the opposite page should be cross-checked as follows:

gross pay
the total of the columns (at the bottom of the form):

basic + overtime + bonus = total gross pay

This should equal the sum of the items in the total gross pay column.

total deductions
the total of the columns (at the bottom of the form):

income tax + NI + pension = total deductions

This should equal the sum of the items in the total deductions column.

net pay
the total of the columns (at the bottom of the form):

total gross pay – total deductions = net pay

This should equal the sum of the items in the net pay column.

Note that the employer's contributions (NI and pension) are not included in this checking process as they are not part of the gross pay calculation.

PAYING WAGES BY CASH

Calculating the net pay is the first part of the payroll process. The wages or salaries then have to be paid. There are a number of different ways of paying:

- by cash
- issuing a cheque
- direct to a bank account by bank giro credit
- direct to an account by electronic transfer (BACS)

We will deal with each of these in turn.

The traditional way of paying wages is by cash, and it is still popular despite the increasing number of people with bank accounts. An employer paying wages in cash can either sub-contract the work to a security firm which will make up the wage packets, or it can be completed by the company's own staff. Preparing wage packets involves collecting sufficient notes and coin from the bank to make up the exact amount for each pay packet. It is normal practice to telephone the bank in advance to tell them the exact denominations of notes and coin needed. Staff collecting this cash from the bank are a obvious target for armed robbery, so common security measures include using two people to collect the money, and for them to vary the route to the bank.

The cash is placed inside a wage packet marked with the name and pay reference or clock number of the employee. Details showing how the payment is made up and the deductions that have been made are provided to each employee. These details can be shown on a separate pay slip or written on the wage packet itself. The office in which this is carried out should be kept secure – for obvious reasons. Employees should sign for the cash wages when they are received.

The total number of notes and coin needed from the bank is worked out on a form known as a *cash analysis*. An important internal security check for the employer is to ensure that the total of the cash analysis is the same as the amount of the cheque given to the bank to cover the wages. A typical cash analysis is illustrated on the next page.

security procedures – unclaimed wages

You will appreciate from what has been explained so far about paying wages in cash that it is a time consuming and therefore expensive procedure:

*   the cash has to be ordered in advance – a very precise order has to be given to the bank
*   the cash has to be transported to the place of work – a security risk
*   the cash has to be stored at the place of work – a further security risk
*   the cash has to be sorted into individual wage packets and checked
*   the cash has to be collected by the employee in person – in some organisations it will have to be signed for

What then if the wage packet is not claimed? Perhaps the employee is off sick or has taken holiday without making arrangements for holiday pay. The employer will have to:

*   make arrangements for the unclaimed wage packet to be kept under lock and key
*   allow the wage packet to be claimed by someone else – but only if that person has written instructions from the employee and proof of identity
*   ensure that whoever collects the wages, signs for them (a book is often kept for this purpose)

why pay cash wages?

You may be wondering why employers continue to pay wages in cash as it is so expensive and inconvenient. There are a number of reasons:

*   employees like cash in hand
*   some employees may not have bank accounts
*   before 1987 it was a legal requirement to pay in cash if employees so wished

cash analysis for week ending..........................

name	£50	£20	£10	£5	£2	£1	50p	20p	10p	5p	2p	1p	total
W Rowberry	1	2	1		2			2		1			104.45
D Stanbury	1	1	1		1	1	1	1	1				83.80
K Peters		2		1	1		1		2		1		47.72
O Robinson	2	2	1	1	1	1		2		1		1	158.46
M Richardson	1	1	2	1			1	1		1	1	1	95.78
NUMBER	5	8	5	3	5	2	3	6	3	3	2	2	
TOTAL (£.p)	250.00	160.00	50.00	15.00	10.00	2.00	1.50	1.20	0.30	0.15	0.04	0.02	490.21

a cash analysis

PAYMENT OF WAGES BY CHEQUE

Another traditional method of payment of wages and salaries is the issue of cheques. This avoids the complexities and security problems involved in the paying of cash wages.

The employee can either cash the cheque at the employer's bank, or, more commonly, pay it into a bank or building society account.

manual and computerised systems

If the employer uses a *manual* payroll system this will involve the person doing the payroll writing out individual cheques made payable to each employee for the net pay earned. This cheque will then be enclosed with the payslip in a sealed envelope.

If a *computerised* payroll system is used, it will commonly print out the payment cheque for each employee, together with the payslip (which may be physically attached to the cheque).

issue of pay cheques – manual payroll

A number of security and authorisation procedures will need to be followed:

- the cheques will need to be kept in a secure place
- the cheques will have to be written out carefully – the details (name, date, words and figures) will have to be checked carefully against the payroll analysis
- the cheques will have to be signed by the required number of authorised signatories (some cheques may be rubber stamped with signatures by authorised staff, or be passed through a 'cheque signing' machine)
- additional checks can include:
  - checking the cheque amounts against the payslips
  - adding up the cheque amounts on a tally-roll calculator and agreeing the total with the payroll analysis total for employees paid by cheque

Although the security risk is not as great as it is with handling cash wages, employers who pay employees by cheque will need to ensure that internal checks exist to prevent staff from fraudulently altering amounts on cheques.

A typical pay cheque is illustrated at the top of the opposite page. Note that:

- the words and figures agree
- lines are drawn after the payee's name and the amount in words – this is to deter fraud
- the cheque is signed by two authorised signatories – directors of the company

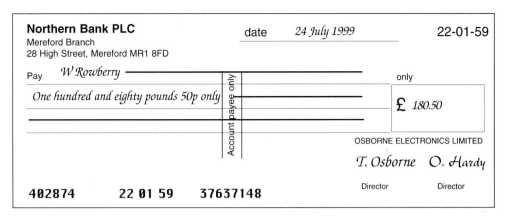

a typical pay cheque

PAYMENT BY BANK GIRO CREDIT

Salaried staff and many weekly-paid employees have their salaries and wages paid directly into their bank or building society account. This reduces the security problems of cash handling by both the employer and the employee. Payments direct to the bank account can be:

- paper based – bank giro credits, *or*
- electronic – BACS

When an employee is paid in this way the employer issues him or her with a payslip – normally in an envelope to preserve confidentiality – but there will obviously be no wage packet.

A bank giro credit (illustrated on the next page) is a piece of paper which is processed through the banking system. It takes three working days to get the money to its destination account, so the employer has to make sure that the bank giro credit is paid in on time.

procedure for processing bank giro credits

The procedure for the payment of the giro credits through the banking system is for the employer to:

- list and total the giro credits on a separate schedule (see page 99)
- to take the credits, schedule and a cheque for the total of all the credits to the bank

These are then processed through the banking system. It is quite common for the employer's computer to work out the net pay, and print out the credits and payslips for the employees. There is no limit to the number of credits that can be paid in: there can be hundreds or more, or as few as two for 'one off' situations such as new employees, as in the Case Study which follows.

CASE STUDY

WAGES BY BANK GIRO CREDIT

Osborne Electronics Ltd pays its employees by cash, cheque, BACS and bank giro credit. In the last week of September 1999 two new employees have their wages paid by bank giro credit. Shown below are:

- the two bank giro credits

- the cheque which covers them (note that it is made payable to the bank where it is paid in – ie Northern Bank, Mereford)

- the schedule which lists the credits

Northern Bank PLC
Mereford Branch
28 High Street, Mereford MR1 8FD

date *25 September* 19 *99*

22-01-59

Pay *Northern Bank PLC* ———————————— only

Five hundred and twenty six pounds only

Account payee only

£ *526.00*

OSBORNE ELECTRONICS LIMITED

T. Osborne   *O. Hardy*

Director   Director

403167   **22 01 59**   **37637148**

---

bank giro credit schedule

to Northern Bank PLC

Branch *Mereford*   Customer account name *Osborne Electronics Limited*
Please distribute the credits listed below. Our cheque for £ *526.00* is enclosed.
signed *O. Hardy*   Director.   Date *25-9-99*

code	bank and branch	account	amount £
40-47-17	Midland Worcester	N E Munney A/c No. 10987652	250.50
20-37-39	Barclays Evestone	B Roke A/c No 98920482	275.50
		TOTAL	526.00

BACS PAYMENTS

Bankers Automated Clearing Services (BACS) is a computer transfer payment system owned by the banks. It is widely used for regular payments such as

- insurance premiums
- settlement of trade debts
- wages and salaries

BACS is a cheap and efficient means of payment because, instead of a piece of paper having to be prepared and despatched, the transfer is set up on a computer file and transferred between the banks' computers – the payment goes direct from account to account.

Sometimes the organisation *receiving* the money will set up the computer data itself (direct debit), sometimes the organisation *sending* the money will set up the computer data, or will get the bank to set it up (standing order/ automated credit).

The payment cycle is three working days. If a business wants its employees to have their money on account on Friday, the money must leave the employer's account on Wednesday. The payment instructions will need to be received by the end of Wednesday, so the payroll department will need to observe this deadline.

payroll through BACS

Payment of wages and salaries through the BACS system can be made in two different ways:

1 The organisation paying the wages and salaries sets up the data on computer file *itself* and sends the data on disk or tape (or direct on-line via BACSTEL) to BACS – this is often the system used by large organisations which have thousands of wages and salary payments to make each week and month. With this system, the organisation's bank is not directly involved, except in that the transfer will pass from the organisation's account.

2 The organisation provides the data to its *bank* which then sets up the computer transfer. This 'automated credit' system requires the organisation to provide the name and banking details of the payees in advance so that the bank can set up the system. When each payroll date approaches the payment details are written on a schedule (see opposite page) and the bank then inputs them into its own computer. This 'automated credit' system is very useful for *smaller* organisations, not only for payroll but also for making payments to suppliers.

CASE STUDY

WAGES BY BACS AUTOMATED CREDIT

City Insurance is an insurance broking firm, based in Mereford. In an attempt to cut administrative costs the Finance Manager has decided to pay employees through the BACS system. The bank has suggested its Auto Credit System. City Insurance has supplied the banking details (sort code and account number) of its employees in advance for the bank to put in its own computer. The weekly pay details are then written on the schedule shown below by City Insurance and sent into the bank on Wednesday 22 September. The employees will be paid on Friday 24 September.

Northern Bank PLC
Auto Credit System

Bank branch... Mereford

Originator name. City Insurance Co ....reference... 07246

Date.. 20-9-99

Branch	Account no	Name	Payee no	Amount
45-45-62	10386394	Smithson H	347	250.00
56-67-23	22347342	Smith M	456	129.76
40-47-07	42472411	Olivier L	209	450.67
76-87-44	56944491	O'Casey S	492	409.79
33-00-77	23442413	French W	385	305.78
59-99-01	46244703	Jones R	546	560.85
		PAYMENT TOTAL		2106.85

Please make the above payments to reach the payees on ...... 24-9-99 ....(date)

Please debit account no...... 37637927 ....with the sum of £... 2106.85 ....

authorised signature...... *S. Laurel* ....

procedures for the schedule

Note that:

- the employer has a reference – 07246 – which is quoted on all instructions

- each employee also a reference number, which is also quoted on all instructions

- the form is totalled to provide the amount which will be taken off the employer's bank account

- the form is signed by an authorised signatory within the organisation – the data cannot be processed without this signature

- it is common for a form of this type to be in two parts: the bank is given the top copy, and the bottom copy is retained by the organisation making payment

It is essential therefore that before the schedule is handed to the bank it is carefully checked for accuracy. The net pay amounts must tally with the figures on the payroll analysis and the authorised signature must be present.

BACS: CONFIDENTIALITY AND SECURITY

confidentiality

Payroll records should be kept confidential. If a person works on payroll and has access to colleagues' pay details, they will undoubtedly be very interesting, but on no account should they be revealed to anyone else, inside or outside the organisation. The only body which will require pay details is the Inland Revenue, as we will see in the next chapter.

security

We have already seen that cash and cheques must be kept securely in order to deter theft. Security measures must also be taken when computer payments are sent. Common frauds include:

- the sending of bogus BACS payments to an employees account

- changing the totals of a large number of payments by a few pence in the hope that the changes will not be noticed – the total difference will then be diverted to an account to which the employee can gain access

These dangers can be overcome by exercising care and caution:

- the individual 'code' issued by BACS to an organisation – without which no payments can be made – should be restricted to a limited number of employees

- payment amounts on the BACS records should be carefully checked against the originals – in the Case Study the net pay amounts were checked against the payroll analysis

CHAPTER SUMMARY

- An employer draws up a payslip for each employee, setting out earnings and deductions.

- An employer may either prepare payslips and payment documentation manually, or on a computer payroll package.

- The details of all employees' earnings and deductions are set out on a payroll analysis sheet, which acts as a useful cross-check for the accuracy of the figures.

- Wages paid by cash involve the employer in ordering the right number of notes and coin from the bank and in making up wage packets.

- The document used for calculating the correct number of notes and coin needed is known as a cash analysis form.

- Wages paid by cheque involve the employer writing out individual cheques which are then issued to employees with the payslips.

- An employer paying wages in cash or by cheque will have to ensure that the cash and cheques are kept secure at all times.

- Wages can be paid direct into a bank or building society account by means of a paper bank giro credit. The employer fills in a giro credit for each payment, lists them on a schedule and issues a cheque to the bank for the overall money total

- The BACS (Bankers Automated Clearing Services) is used to make computer transfers of wages and salaries from the bank account of the employer to the account of each employee.

- In order to originate a BACS payment the employer will either set up a BACS tape or disk or will give the payment details to the bank so that the bank can originate the payments.

- An employer must ensure that BACS payments are checked carefully and that payment security procedures are adhered to in order to deter fraud.

KEY TERMS

payslip	advice showing earnings and deductions from pay
payroll analysis sheet	summary or 'master' sheet showing all the figures produced when payroll is processed; also useful as a cross-checking device for accuracy of figures
cash analysis	a form setting out the details of notes and coin needed from the bank by an employer when paying wages in cash
bank giro credit	paper document used for making payments – including wages and salaries – through the banking system
giro credit schedule	a schedule listing and totalling bank giro credits being paid through the banking system
BACS	Bankers Automated Clearing Services, a company owned by the banks, established to process computerised transfers between banks
BACSTEL	an on-line (BACS by telephone) service for processing BACS payments – the telephone link is between banks and their customers

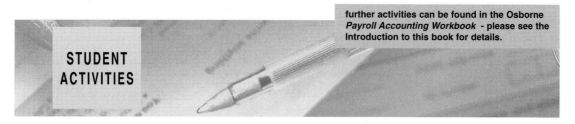

further activities can be found in the Osborne *Payroll Accounting Workbook* - please see the Introduction to this book for details.

STUDENT ACTIVITIES

7.1   Examine the payslip shown below and answer the questions that follow.

OSBORNE ELECTRONICS LTD		Pay Advice	Week 2
payments		**deductions**	
	£		£
Basic pay	180.00	Income tax	51.11
Overtime	80.00	National Insurance	25.45
Bonus	60.00	Superannuation	9.00
TOTAL GROSS PAY	320.00	SAYE	00.00
		TOTAL DEDUCTIONS	85.56
Gross pay to date	620.00		
Taxable pay to date	446.26	TOTAL NET PAY	234.44
Date	**Employee**	Income tax to date	97.61
16.04.99	J Smithers	National Insurance to date	48.90

(a)   What was J Smithers' gross pay in week 1 of the tax year?

(b)   Are there any essential payslip details missing?

(c)   What details are missing? Does it matter?

(d)   What percentage of basic pay does J Smithers contribute as a pension payment?

7.2   A new member of staff working on payroll asks

"Why do we have to fill in a payroll analysis sheet? Surely we have got all the information we need on the P11 and on the payslip."

What would be your reply?

7.3   Rule up and complete a payroll sheet from the following details of weekly pay:

	A Lucas	D Hunt	I Atkins	C Robbins
	£	£	£	£
Basic pay	110.00	110.00	110.00	110.00
Overtime	13.75	-	13.75	6.88
Bonus	10.00	10.00	10.00	10.00
Income tax	13.75	15.00	13.50	10.25
National Insurance (employee)	9.02	7.79	9.02	8.40
National Insurance (employer)	12.01	10.84	12.01	11.38
Savings	1.20	1.20	1.20	1.20

7.4 From your answer to question 7.3 prepare a cash analysis. The payroll office has the following standing instructions for making up wage packets:

PAY PACKETS

1 Each employee's pay packet is to be made up in the highest value bank notes and coin available.
2 No bank notes <u>in excess of £20</u> are to be used.

7.5 State three disadvantages of paying wages by cash.

7.6 Bill, who is paid in cash, is off sick on pay day. What procedures would you follow to ensure that Bill gets his money?

7.7 State three disadvantages of paying wages by cheque.

7.8 A new employee, who is paid by cheque, queries her pay cheque on her first pay day:

"This cheque hasn't been signed properly; it has only got two rubber stamped signatures on it. I thought that a cheque had to be signed in ink. Will my bank accept it?"

What would be your reply?

7.9 Your payroll office has thirty weekly-paid employees paid by bank giro credit. The pay day is Friday. Draw up a list of instructions, including timing, setting out how the payments are prepared and processed. Assume that you have

- a payroll analysis giving net pay for each employee – this has been checked already

- the banking details of each employee in the individual employee payroll record files

7.10 What method of payment would you recommend for the payroll systems of the following businesses? Give reasons in each case.

(a) a fully computerised insurance company with 1,200 staff on its books

(b) a firm of solicitors with fifteen employees but no computers, apart from word processors

(c) a sole trader builder who employs two workers who do not have bank accounts

Your choice should be based on the cheapest and most convenient alternative. Choose from: cash wages, cheque payment, bank giro credit, automated credit (manually completed schedule for BACS input by the bank), direct BACS (tape/disk).

8 SENDING PAYMENTS AND RETURNS

this chapter covers . . .

The employer operates the payroll system – calculates gross pay, calculates the deductions and ensures that the employees receive the correct amount of net pay on the due date.

As we will see in this chapter, it is also the duty of the employer to ensure that:

- the income tax and National Insurance deducted through the PAYE system are paid to the Inland Revenue by the due date on the correct form – a P30B

- payroll records are accurately maintained so that at the end of the tax year employees can be given a summary of their pay and PAYE deductions – on a P60

- at the end of the tax year the Inland Revenue is sent a summary of the PAYE deductions for all employees – on a Form P35

- records are kept for deductions made to other external agencies, eg pension funds, savings institutions (for SAYE) and the Charities Aid Foundation (for GAYE)

NVQ PERFORMANCE CRITERIA COVERED

unit 3: RECORDING PAYROLL TRANSACTIONS

element 3

make authorised payments, claims and returns to external agencies

- ❏ due payments , claims and returns are correct and made within specified deadlines
- ❏ relevant returns and documents are correctly prepared and submitted to external agencies in good time
- ❏ the deduction records reconcile with the payroll system
- ❏ queries relating to external agencies are dealt with promptly, courteously and effectively
- ❏ documentation is correctly filed
- ❏ safety and security procedures for the handling of cash and cheques are followed
- ❏ confidentiality and security of information is maintained
- ❏ the organisation's policies, regulations, procedures and timescales are followed
- ❏ discrepancies, unusual features or queries are identified and referred to the appropriate person or resolved

PAYE RETURNS – AN OVERVIEW

This chapter will explain, using text and diagrams, the PAYE payment and returns process. Read the text carefully and then study the diagrams and the illustrations of the forms that are used.

payment of income tax and National Insurance

As we have already seen in this book, organisations operating PAYE pay the deductions collected to the Inland Revenue on a regular basis. For most organisations this means a monthly payment. The money must be sent within fourteen days of the end of the tax month, using a P30B payslip. As the tax month ends on the 5th, this means that the money must by sent by the 19th.

'Small' employers, who send small amounts of PAYE deductions, can choose to pay quarterly: for the tax quarters ending on 5 July, 5 October, 5 January and 5 April. Whatever the payment interval, the payments will comprise:

	income tax collected from employees – deducted from their gross pay
plus	**employees' National Insurance contributions** – deducted from their gross pay
plus	**employer's National Insurance contributions** – paid by the employer and not deducted from employees' pay
less	any payments *reclaimable* from the Inland Revenue (eg tax refunds, Statutory Sick Pay, Statutory Maternity Pay, NI 'Holidays', NI rebates)

The data for these payments

- is first calculated for individual employees on the P11 deductions working sheet

- is then

  - *either* transferred to a yellow summary sheet P32 , *or*

  - transferred to the front of the P30B payslip booklet (where a summary is provided)

- is then transferred to the payslip P30B for the appropriate month in the payslip booklet (this is a chequebook-sized book of bank giro credits used for paying the money to the Inland Revenue)

payment of PAYE deductions

The money is then paid, normally using the bank giro credit system. The giro is paid into the bank with a covering cheque. It is also possible to pay by post, Girobank, through the Post Office, or by BACS (by arrangement with the Inland Revenue). Most employers use the bank giro credits provided – the P30Bs.

Now look at the diagram below which summarises the month-end (or quarter-end) procedure for a small business with three employees. Examples of the documents are also shown.

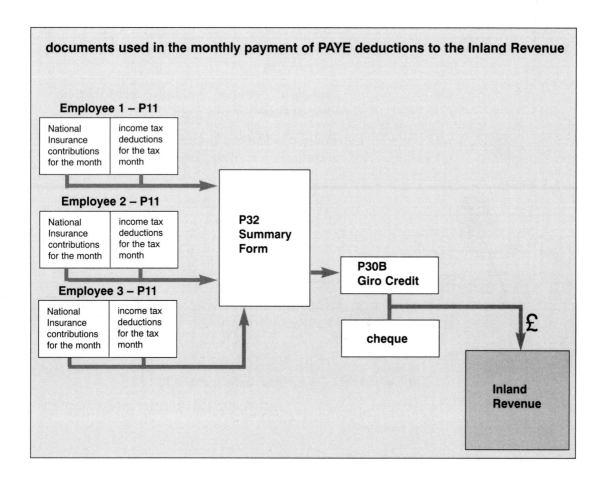

documents used in the monthly payment of PAYE deductions to the Inland Revenue

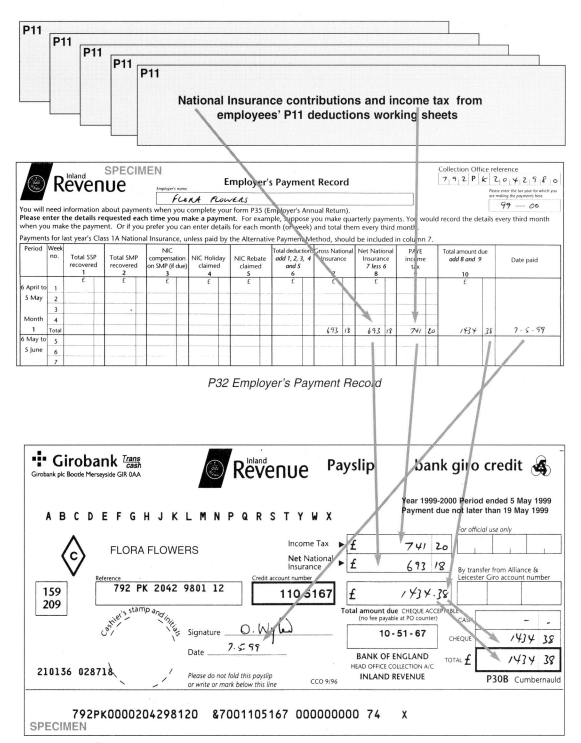

P32 Employer's Payment Record

P30B Inland Revenue Payslip

end of tax year procedures

At the end of each tax year (ie after 5 April) the employer will:

- total up the deduction and pay columns on the P11s:
  - gross pay
  - income tax paid
  - National Insurance contribution columns (the employee's National Insurance contributions and total National Insurance contributions [the employee's and employer's])
  - any Statutory Sick Pay and Statutory Maternity Pay, and any Statutory Maternity Pay recovered

- complete the total boxes at the bottom of the P11 for
  - National Insurance Contribution columns
  - pay and tax (split between previous and present employment - see page 112)

- prepare a summary of these totals for each employee on form P14 (which comes in 3 parts)

- give the bottom copy of the P14 (the copy is the P60) to each employee who is still working for the employer, by 31 May of the tax year

- transfer the totals of the P14s to the employer's annual return to the Inland Revenue – the P35

- send the completed P35, plus the P14s, to the tax office by 19 May; the Inland Revenue will keep one copy of the P14, the other copy will go to the Department of Social Security

- make sure that the P14s are photocopied before they leave the office – there is no employer's copy in the three-part form!

P11D and P9D

In addition, at the end of the tax year the employer must send forms P11D and P9D to the Inland Revenue where necessary by 6 July. These list taxable benefits and expenses received by an employee, eg a company car, petrol, a mobile phone, and so on. These are normally taxed through an adjustment in the employee's tax code – ie the code will be reduced, or even become a K (negative) code.

You do not have to study the form P11D or P9D for your NVQ Level 2 assessment, but you should be aware what they are and what they do.

Now study the diagram on the opposite page and the forms on the pages that follow.

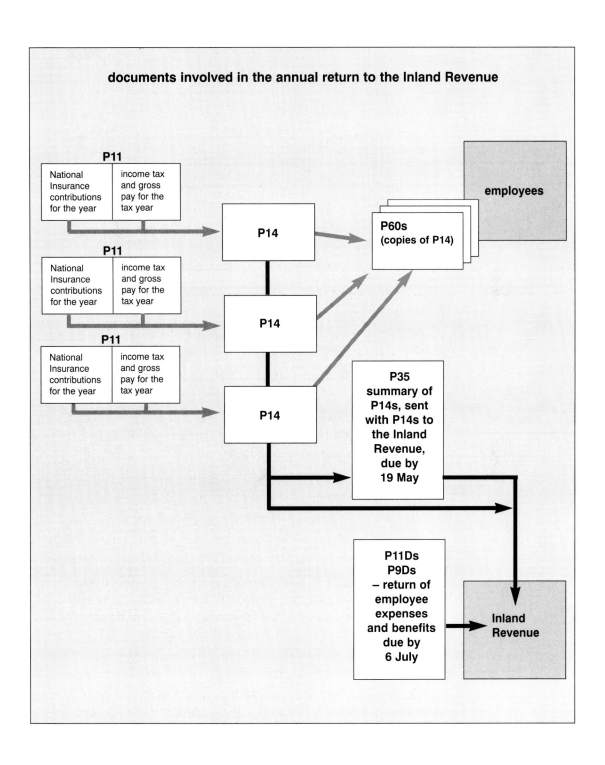

documents involved in the annual return to the Inland Revenue

P11

National Insurance contributions for the year	income tax and gross pay for the tax year

P11

National Insurance contributions for the year	income tax and gross pay for the tax year

P11

National Insurance contributions for the year	income tax and gross pay for the tax year

P14

P14

P14

employees

P60s (copies of P14)

P35 summary of P14s, sent with P14s to the Inland Revenue, due by 19 May

P11Ds P9Ds – return of employee expenses and benefits due by 6 July

Inland Revenue

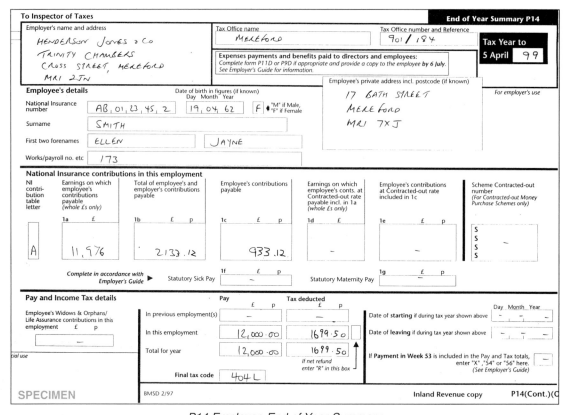

P14 Employee End of Year Summary

completing the P14

- the form should be completed using a ball point pen so that the details appear clearly on all three copies

- the employee's National Insurance number must be correct

- the employer's tax district and reference number must be recorded accurately – if in doubt, look at the P35, where the details are preprinted

- quote the employee's full names (they should be on the P11)

- in the National Insurance section make sure that the contribution table letter is shown in the left-hand column; the figures in the other columns will be taken from the total boxes on the bottom of the P11

- include Statutory Sick Pay and Statutory Maternity Pay (show the total SSP for all tax months when SSP has been recovered)

- the 'Total for Year' includes gross pay and tax relating to this and any previous employment (details of pay and tax for previous employment will be found on the P45 brought by the employee)

- the final tax code used (on 5 April) will be entered in the box at the bottom of the form

Inland Revenue

Employer's Annual Return

Year ended 5 April 19 99

Your reference _____

Tax Office reference ___ 084 / 175

Tax Office telephone number ___ 0172 76310 4

Return to:

ENIGMA MUSIC LTD
JAEGER HOUSE
BASSINGTON ROAD
MEREFORD
MR7 OTE

HM INSPECTOR OF TAXES
MEREFORD DISTRICT 2
BLOCK 17
GOVERNMENT OFFICES
HELSTON RD, MEREFORD

Accounts Office reference ___ 084 OZ ZO4Z 970 1

PAYE Income Tax and National Insurance contributions

This form will help check that you have made the right PAYE payments during the year. Please see your *Employer's Quick Guide to PAYE and NICs* (CWG1 cards) for guidance, or contact your Tax Office if you need help. **You are required by law to:**

- complete and sign this form, and **send it in time to reach the Tax Office by 19 May** following the end of the tax year
- send with this form the DSS and Inland Revenue copies of the *End of Year Summary* (**new style** form P14) for each employee you were required to complete a *Deductions Working Sheet* (form P11) for during the year.

Penalties are chargeable where a return is late. We will charge these automatically if the return for the year ended 5 April 1998 is received after 26 May 1998.

Checklist

Tick the boxes – you must answer each question

1 Have you enclosed an *End of Year Summary* (form P14) or a form P38(S) for every person in your paid employment, either on a casual basis or otherwise, during the above tax year?
If no, please submit an *Employer's Supplementary Return* (form P38A).
No ✓   Yes ☐

2 Did you make any "free of tax" payments to any employee? In other words, did you bear any of the tax yourself rather than deduct it from the employee?
No ✓   Yes ☐

3 So far as you know, did anyone else pay expenses or provide benefits or vouchers exchangeable for money, goods or services to any of your employees because they were employed by you during the year?
No ✓   Yes ☐

4 Did anyone employed by a person or company outside the UK work for you in the UK for 30 or more days in a row?
No ✓   Yes ☐

If yes, have you included them in the list on the back of this form or on any continuation sheets?
No -   Yes -

5 Have you paid any of an employee's pay to someone other than that employee? (for example, to a school)?
No ✓   Yes ☐

If yes, have you included it in the payments shown on that employee's *End of Year Summary* (form P14)?
No -   Yes -

Declaration and Certificate

Tick one box for each item

This declaration and certificate covers any documents authorised by the Inland Revenue as substitutes for the forms mentioned below.

I declare and certify that for the above tax year

- an *End of Year Summary* (form P14) is enclosed for each employee or director for whom I was required to complete a *Deductions Working Sheet* (form P11) during the year ✓

- completed *Employer's Supplementary Returns* (forms P38A)
  are enclosed ✓   are not due ☐

- completed *Returns of expenses payments and benefits* (forms P11D and
  are enclosed ✓   will be sent later ☐   are not due ☐   P11D(b)) *

- completed *Returns of Expenses Payments and Income from which Tax Cannot be Deducted* (form P9D) for employees earning at a rate of less than £8,500 per annum *
  are enclosed -   will be sent later -   are not due -

All the details on this form and any forms enclosed are fully and truly stated to the best of my knowledge and belief

Signature of employer

E. Nagle   E. NAGLE

Capacity in which signed   Date
MANAGING DIRECTOR   12.05.99

You may be penalised or prosecuted if you make false statements

* If you are a new employer we may not have sent you any forms P11D or P9D. If you are paying expenses or providing benefits please refer to the *Employer's Further Guide to PAYE and NICs* (booklet CWG2). Ask your Tax Office for these forms if you need them.

Please turn over

SPECIMEN

P35 (Man.)

26786 11.97 Niceday Stationery & Print Limited   BMSD10/97   W0K0023

P35 Employer End of Year Summary (front)

Deductions Working Sheets

List here the individual *Deductions Working Sheets* (forms P11) which you have filled in during the year and which contain a figure under either of the headings shown.

If there is not enough space here to list all your employees please prepare continuation sheets.

Enter only the figures for 'this employment'

Employee's name — Put an asterisk (*) beside the name if the person is a director	National Insurance contributions (NIC) — Enter the total of employee's and employer's NIC †	Income tax deducted or refunded — Write 'R' beside amount to show a net refund
EDWARD RAGLE *	£ 4560 —	£ 4908 .
PENNY RAGLE *	£ — .	£ 600 —
JAMES LOCKHART	£ 1200 82	£ 1057 44
OLIVIA PERRY	£ 1081 95	£ 898 56
RASHID PATEL	£ 330 33	£ 371 36
HELEN O'TROY	£ — .	£ 168 —
	£	£
EDWARD RAGLE CLASS 1A	£ 651 98	£
	£ .	£
	£	£
	£ 7825 08	£ 8003 36

† Include Class 1A contributions payable in the year, unless you paid these by the Alternative Payment Method.

Note: the columns for **SSP and SMP paid** have been discontinued, but the figures may still appear on some computer-printed continuation sheets. If so, please ignore them.

Calculation of NIC and Income Tax now due

National Insurance contributions (NIC)		*Remember to deduct amounts marked "R"* Income Tax	
Total from this page	A £ 7825 08	Total from this page	N £ 8003 36
Totals from continuation sheets	B £ — —	Totals from continuation sheets	O £ — —
Total NIC A + B	C £ 7825 08	**Total tax** N + O	P £ 8003 36
Received from Inland Revenue to pay SSP / SMP	D £ — —	Received from Inland Revenue to refund tax	Q £
C + D	E £ 7825 08	Tax deducted from sub-contractors see your *Contractor's Statement* (form SC35)	R £
Statutory Sick Pay **recovered**	F £ — —	P + Q + R	S £ 8003 36
Statutory Maternity Pay **recovered**	G £ — —	Tax already paid	T £ 8003 36
NIC compensation on SMP see your payment record	H £ — —	**Tax now due** S – T	U £ NIL
NIC Holiday claimed	I £ — —		
F + G + H + I	J £ — —		
Total NIC payable to Accounts Office E – J	K £ 7825 08		
NIC already paid	L £ 7825 08		
NIC now due K – L	M £ NIL		

Do not send payment with this form. Send it to the Inland Revenue Accounts Office immediately. See notes overleaf.

Contracted-out pension schemes

Enter here your employer's contracting-out number, where applicable:

[—]

(You will find the number on the Occupational Pensions Board's Certificate)

§ I claim payment under Section 7 of the Social Security Act 1986 for each employee on whose *End of Year Summary* (form P14) I have entered a scheme contracting-out number. So far as I know, none of these employees is in an employment which has been contracted-out by reference to any other scheme since 1 January 1986.

"√" [ ]

§ You can only claim if this form is used for 1992-93 or earlier

SPECIMEN

P35 Employer End of Year Summary (back)

functions of the P35, the employer's annual return

Remember that the P35 is a *summary* form which acts as a covering document for other forms returned to the Inland Revenue – including P14, P11D and P9D. The P38(A) – which records details of casual workers – should also be returned with the P35. The forms must be returned by 19 May.

The P35 also acts as an *arithmetic checklist* which ensures that *the right PAYE payments have been made*. If the employer finds that too little has been paid, the amount will be recorded on the P35 and paid separately to the Inland Revenue.

P35 – front

- the P35 normally arrives from the Inland Revenue with the employer's details preprinted
- there are various check boxes on the front of the form which must be completed as appropriate – if you read them through you will see that they are self-explanatory
- the employer has to sign a declaration stating that the details on the P35 and any enclosed form are correct (to the best of the employer's knowledge)

P35 – back – P14 summary

- the top part of the form is used to list the employees and the total employer/employee National Insurance and income tax deductions
- the details should be taken direct from the P14s enclosed with the P35
- company directors should be listed first (alphabetically) and asterisked*
- other employees should be listed after directors and in alphabetical order
- if there is not enough room on the form, employees can be listed on continuation sheets
- the P14s should be enclosed in the same order as the listing

P35 – back – calculation of NIC and income tax due

- the remaining part of the form calculates the totals of National Insurance contributions and income tax due and compares them with the actual amounts paid; any shortfall should be paid to the Inland Revenue without delay (a payslip for this is provided in the P30B payslip booklet)
- details for this part of the form can be taken from the P11s, or more easily, from the P32 employer's summary form
- this part of the form provides a useful check that the totals of the P14s reconciles with the totals from the payroll records (P32 or P11s) – in other words, it will pick up any errors on the P14s

RETURNS TO OTHER OUTSIDE AGENCIES

Although the regular returns to the Inland Revenue are very important, the person or department dealing with payroll must also ensure that records are kept of amounts paid to other external agencies, and returns are made as and when required, using the correct forms.

Payment of the deductions will clearly be amalgamated in one lump sum, so the recipient of the money, whether it be a pension provider or a charity, will need to know on a separate schedule *who* has contributed *what,* so that the necessary accounting entries can be made. Examples of this include:

GAYE

Charitable donations made through the Give As You Earn (GAYE) scheme involve deductions made from gross pay each time the payroll is run. Details of these deductions – employee names and amounts – will be regularly sent to the collecting agency, eg the Charities Aid Foundation.

SAYE

Save As You Earn deductions will be paid and advised to the appropriate savings institution each time the payroll is run.

pension contributions and AVCs

Pensions providers – and here we mean companies that provide personal pensions, company pension schemes and AVCs (Additional Voluntary Contributions) – will need to adjust the pension or AVC scheme of the employee each time a payment is made.

CHAPTER SUMMARY

• Employers must make a regular payment of PAYE deductions (normally monthly) to the Inland Revenue on a P30B payslip.

• The PAYE payments comprise National Insurance contributions *plus* income tax *less* any amounts reclaimable such as income tax refunds and Statutory Sick Pay and Statutory Maternity Pay.

• The calculation of these payments is normally carried out by transferring the individual P11 amounts to a P32 summary sheet, where they are totalled.

• Payment of PAYE deductions is usually made through the banking system, by bank giro (the P30B) or by BACS computer transfer.

- Form P14 (which comes in three parts) is used to make an annual return of pay, National Insurance contributions and income tax for each individual employee to the Inland Revenue and the Department of Social Security.

- The details for each P14 are taken from the total boxes on the employee's P11 deductions working sheet and the P45 (if there is one).

- The bottom part of the P14 is given to the employee by the 31 May and is known as the P60.

- The P14s are sent to the Inland Revenue by 19 May annually, together with a P35 summary sheet.

- The P35 lists and totals the amounts of National Insurance and income tax from the individual P14s. It also acts a checklist to ensure that the employer has completed all the necessary employee tax forms and has deducted the correct amounts of National Insurance and income tax.

- The payroll function in a business must also make payments and returns to other external bodies in respect of deductions from gross pay, to pension funds and charitable bodies, for example.

**KEY
TERMS**

P11 — the Inland Revenue form used for calculating each employee's National Insurance contributions and income tax every time the payroll is run; it is totalled up at the end of each tax year to provide the figures for the P14/P60 (see below)

P32 — the Inland Revenue yellow summary form onto which are transferred the *totals* of National Insurance contributions and income tax for all employees each time the payroll is run; it provides the totals for the regular payments of deductions to the Inland Revenue on the P30B payslip

P30B — the payslip (in the form of a bank giro credit) used to pay National Insurance contributions and income tax for all employees to the Inland Revenue, normally by the 19th of each month (but quarterly for 'small' employers)

P14 — the annual summary of each employee's pay, National Insurance contributions and income tax; it comes in 3 parts:

• Part 1 goes to the Department of Social Security

• Part 2 goes to the Inland Revenue

• Part 3 goes to the employee - this is the P60

Parts 1 and 2 are initially sent by the employer to the Inland Revenue with the P35 (see below)

P35	the Inland Revenue summary form completed by the employer at the end of each tax year, summarising the P14s and advising the total PAYE deductions
P11D & P9D	the Inland Revenue forms used to report to the Inland Revenue any taxable benefits and expenses received by employees during the tax year (the P11D is used for directors and more highly paid employees) – they are due by 6 July annually

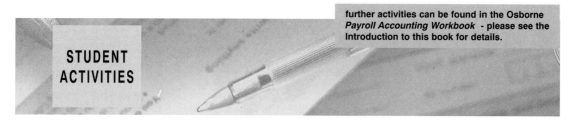

further activities can be found in the Osborne *Payroll Accounting Workbook* **- please see the Introduction to this book for details.**

STUDENT ACTIVITIES

8.1 Payment of employees' PAYE deductions must in all cases be made to the Inland Revenue by the 19th of the month.

True or false?

8.2 Payment to the Inland Revenue is made using:
(a) P45
(b) P46
(c) P30B
(d) P11D

Choose one of the options shown above.

8.3 Draw up a summary sheet, suitable for new entrants to a payroll department, explaining *in simple terms* the function of the following forms:
(a) P11
(b) P32
(c) P30B
(d) P14
(e) P35
(f) P11D

8.4 You are completing a P14 for an employee who joined your firm last June.

(a) Where would you find the figures for pay and tax for the previous employment?

(b) Why would you not have to worry about National Insurance contributions made in the previous employment?

8.5   You are processing the payroll for Angelo Design Consultancy, a small firm with 4 employees, all on monthly pay and all of whom have worked for the firm for the whole tax year. It is Month 12 of the tax year and the figures from the employees' P11s are as follows:

employee	pay	NIC	NIC	income tax
	(for month)	*(employer & employee)*	*(employee only)*	*(for month)*
	£	£	£	£
Mike L Angelo	1,200	218.28	98.38	188.14
Leo Nardo	1,000	178.28	78.38	167.50
Budd E Celli	1,100	198.28	88.38	178.45
Matt Ease	950	168.68	73.58	157.80

(a)   What are the totals which will be recorded on the P32 summary sheet for Month 12?

(b)   What will be the amounts recorded on the P30B payslip for Month 12?

8.6   It is the end of the tax year and you are preparing the annual return to the Inland Revenue for the Angelo Design Consultancy (which featured in question 8.5). You have totalled up the columns on the P11s and have the following results:

employee	pay	NIC	NIC	income tax
		(employer & employee)	*(employee only)*	*(for month)*
	£	£	£	£
Mike L Angelo	14,400	2,619.36	1,180.56	2,257.68
Leo Nardo	12,000	2,139.36	940.56	2,010.00
Budd E Celli	13,200	2,379.36	1,060.56	2,141.40
Matt Ease	11,400	2,024.16	882.96	1,893.60

(a)   What figures from the P11 totals will be recorded on the employees' P14s?

(b)   What figures from the P14s will be recorded on the P35?

(c)   When the P35 is being completed, you find that the totals on the P32 do not agree with the totalled up PAYE deductions on the P35. The totals on the P32 are: net NICs paid £8,993.56 and income tax paid £8,144.80. What do you think has happened? How would you put things right?

9 PAYROLL AND THE ACCOUNTING SYSTEM

this chapter covers . . .

So far in this book we have looked at the practicalities of operating payroll – calculating the gross and net pay of employees, paying wages and salaries and completing returns to outside agencies.

In this chapter we turn to the recording of the payroll transactions in the double-entry accounting system of an organisation. This is needed for

- providing an overall figure for management – eg the total wage and salary cost of the organisation for an accounting period

- analysis of the labour costs of different areas of the business, eg different departments, products, and seeing how they compare with budgeted labour costs

- confirming the accuracy of the payroll totals – for gross pay, amounts due to the Inland Revenue, to pension funds and other external agencies

NVQ PERFORMANCE CRITERIA COVERED

unit 3: RECORDING PAYROLL TRANSACTIONS

element 1

operate and maintain a payroll accounting system

❑ a summary and analysis of the payroll is accurately transferred to the correct ledger accounts

❑ confidentiality and security of information is maintained

❑ the organisation's procedures and timescales are observed

❑ discrepancies, unusual features or queries are identified and referred to the appropriate person or resolved

PAYROLL AND THE DOUBLE-ENTRY ACCOUNTING SYSTEM

types of accounting system

You will be familiar with the double-entry accounting system from your study of cash and credit accounting. If you have not studied and practised double-entry accounting, or if you feel unsure about the subject, you are advised to study Osborne Books' *Cash & Credit Accounting Tutorial,* chapters 4, 8 and 10 before proceeding any further with this chapter.

Payroll accounting systems will either be paper-based, or computerised. Many 'off-the-shelf' computer accounting packages are now available, such as the widely-used Sage™ programs. You will doubtless be looking at computerised accounting elsewhere in your studies. In this chapter, however, we will use a paper-based system to illustrate the entries generated by the operation of payroll so that you will understand the double-entry principles involved.

types of accounts used

Wages and salaries are a major *expense* for any organisation, but remember that the net pay received by employees is not the same as the *gross pay*, the expense to the employer. The wages and salaries expenses figure that appears in the profit statement of the organisation will be the result of a number of adjustments:

* calculated in the payroll process
* entered in the double-entry accounts of the organisation

There is no 'hard-and-fast' rule which states what accounts have to be set up. The accounts used in this chapter are fairly typical, but you may well find that practice varies in different organisations. The main accounts to be used will be in the cash book (for bank transactions) and the nominal ledger (expenses).

The types of transaction which need entering in the accounts include:

* income tax collected by the employer under PAYE and paid to the Inland Revenue by the 19th of the month *after* the payroll has been processed
* employees' National Insurance contributions collected by the employer under PAYE and paid to the Inland Revenue by the 19th of the month *after* the payroll has been processed
* employer's National Insurance contributions paid to the Inland Revenue
* employees' pension contributions deducted from employees' pay and paid to pension funds

- pension contributions provided by the *employer* and paid to pension funds

The double-entry accounts commonly used include:

Bank this is in the cash book and records:

- payment of cash wages, wages cheques and BACS wages transfers – ie the *net pay* of employees
- payment of cheques to outside agencies, eg the monthly payment of deductions to the Inland Revenue and payments to pension funds

Wages & Salaries this is in the nominal ledger and records:

- employees' *gross pay*
- employer's National Insurance contributions
- employer's pension contributions (if there are any)

- in short, it is the *expense* account for paying employees

Inland Revenue this is in the nominal ledger and records amounts payable to the Inland Revenue (PAYE deductions)

Pension Fund this is in the nominal ledger and records amounts payable to external pension funds: the employer's and employees' contributions (as appropriate to the type of pension)

A common practice is to put all the entries through a Wages and Salaries Control account.

wages and salaries control account

You will probably have studied the *control accounts* used by organisations for purchases and sales. They are covered in Osborne Books' *Cash & Credit Accounting Tutorial,* chapter 10.

A *control account* is a 'master' account which 'controls' a number of other subsidiary ledger accounts. It is used to record the total of transactions passing through the subsidiary accounts. The balance of the control account should always be equal to the total balances of the subsidiary accounts.

Thus the sales ledger control account will give the total of the debtors of an organisation and the purchases ledger control account will give the total of the creditors. This provides useful information to the management: they will be able to see how much the organisation is owed by debtors and the amount it owes to creditors.

A *wages and salaries control account* is also a master account: all the entries to the various accounts set up to deal with payroll transactions pass through the control account.

The diagram below shows the structure of the control account and subsidiary accounts. Note that the bank account is not shown here – it is involved in many of the transactions, as we will see in the Case Study which follows, but it is not strictly speaking 'subsidiary'.

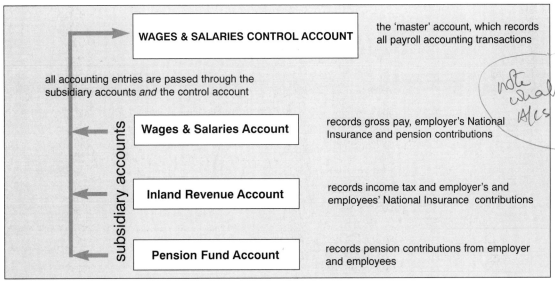

Wages & Salaries control account and subsidiary accounts

CASE STUDY

FLUFFIES: WAGES & SALARIES CONTROL ACCOUNT

Fluffies is a small knitwear business employing five staff. It operates a monthly payroll which is run on the last day of the month. Payroll figures for November are:

gross pay	£5,500
net pay received by employees	£3,875
income tax deducted by PAYE	£900
NIC (employees' contribution)	£450
NIC (employer's contribution)	£550
pension: paid by the employees by deduction from pay	£275
pension: employer's contribution	£275

What are the payments that are due, and to whom are they payable?

payments due to the Inland Revenue

Income tax deducted from employees' pay	£900
Employees' National Insurance contributions	£450
Employer's National Insurance contributions	£550
	£1,900

payments due to the pension fund, Allied Life PLC

Employees' contributions, deducted from pay	£275
Employer's contributions	£275
	£550

payments due to the employees

Gross pay	£5,500	
less		
Income tax	£900	
National Insurance	£450	
Pension contributions	£275	
Net pay due		£3,875

payments total

	£6,325

These four amounts, shown here in the right-hand column, are recorded in the payroll records and have to be entered into the ledger accounts. This is done as follows:

Step 1

Transfer the total of the payments (here £6,325) to Wages and Salaries Account (this is the cost to the employer) and to Wages & Salaries Control Account

debit Wages & Salaries Account
credit Wages & Salaries Control Account

Dr	**Wages & Salaries Account**	Cr
	£	£
30 Nov Wages & salaries 6,325		

The side text reads: FLUFFIES: WAGES & SALARIES CONTROL ACCOUNT

Dr		Wages & Salaries Control Account		Cr
	£			£
		30 Nov Wages & salaries		6,325

You will see that this total agrees with the *total monthly payroll expense to the business*: gross pay (£5,500) *plus* employer's National Insurance (£550) *plus* employer's pension contribution (£275) *equals* £6,325.

Step 2
Make entries for the payment of wages (the net pay paid from the bank)

debit Wages & Salaries Control Account
credit Bank Account

Dr		Wages & Salaries Control Account		Cr
	£			£
30 Nov Bank	3,875	30 Nov Wages & salaries		6,325

Dr		Bank Account		Cr
	£			£
		30 Nov Wages & Salaries Control Account		3,875

Step 3
Transfer the amount due to the Inland Revenue to the Inland Revenue Account

debit Wages & Salaries Control Account
credit Inland Revenue Account (which will become a 'creditor' account until the amount is paid in December and 'clears' the account back to zero)

The 'amount due' is £1,900 and comprises income tax (£900) and National Insurance contributions (employer's [£550] and employees' [£450]).

Dr		Wages & Salaries Control Account		Cr
	£			£
30 Nov Bank	3,875	30 Nov Wages & salaries		6,325
30 Nov Inland Revenue	1,900			

Dr   **Inland Revenue Account**   Cr

	£		£
		30 Nov Wages & Salaries	
		Control Account	1,900

Step 4

Transfer the amount due to the pension fund, Allied Life PLC

The amount due is £550 (employer's contribution £275, employee's contribution £275)

debit   Wages & Salaries Control Account
credit   Pension Fund Account (which will become a 'creditor' account until the
                 amount is paid in December and 'clears' the account back to zero)

Dr   **Wages & Salaries Control Account**   Cr

		£		£
30 Nov	Bank	3,875	30 Nov Wages & salaries	6,325
30 Nov	Inland Revenue	1,900		
30 Nov	Pension Fund	550		
		6,325		6,325

Dr   **Pension Fund Account**   Cr

	£		£
		30 Nov Wages & Salaries	
		Control Account	550

conclusion

You will see from the double-entry book-keeping entries shown above that the Wages & Salaries Control Account acts as a 'master' account for all the payroll accounting transactions carried out each time the payroll is run. At the end of the process the control account balance reverts to zero – you will see above that the total of both sides after the pension fund transfer is £6,325 – ie the balance is nil.

The double-entry book-keeping also shows:

- *Wages & Salaries Account:* the cumulative cost during the year of paying the employees – this includes the gross pay, employer's National Insurance and any pension contributions paid by the employer; this is the figure that will appear in the organisation's profit statement – it is the expense borne by the employer

- in the *Inland Revenue Account* and *Pension Fund Account* any amounts owing – for example at the end of the month before payments are passed to these agencies – these will be *creditor* accounts and will feature as current liabilities (amounts owing in the short term) in any balance sheet that is drawn up at the end of the month

PAYROLL AND COSTING

labour as a cost

Wages and salaries – known as *labour costs* – are a major item of expense for any organisation. Most organisations will *budget* for an estimated level of expenditure on wages and salaries, and monitor how well expenditure is keeping to budget during the financial year.

For the organisation with a small workforce, eg a shop or an office, this is fairly straightforward – the balance of the wages and salaries account will tell the owner(s) how much has been spent to date.

For the larger business, eg a manufacturer or retailer employing hundreds of staff, the top management will need to keep a close eye on how well *each part of the business* is performing and keeping to budget. The management will need to look critically at the *labour cost* of a number of different areas of the business:

departments   Each department in the organisation – eg sales, purchasing, administration, finance, distribution – is likely to have a separate staffing budget, eg £55,000 a month, to which the departmental manager will have to adhere – so he/she will have to keep an eye on efficiency and issues such as overtime worked.

products   A manufacturer is likely to build into each product a *labour cost*; a car manufacturer, for example, will calculate from observation and experience the amount of time it takes to assemble a certain make of car – so the production manager (or team) will watch carefully the time taken to produce each vehicle.

recording of payroll – coding

You may well ask how the payroll process can help to monitor labour costs. This is normally achieved by *coding* employees and operations, so that labour costs can be calculated easily, particularly if a computer payroll system is used. This is best explained by looking at examples.

departmental code Each department in the organisation is likely to have a specific code; employees who work in a department are given that code so that when their wages and salaries are processed through the accounting system, that expense is allocated to the correct department.

job code   Some organisations – for example professional firms of accountants and solicitors – allocate a specific code to each job or client, so that the time spent on that job or client's work, whoever does it, is accurately logged and charged by means of a job sheet.

reconciling gross pay to total labour costing

One task when working on payroll is to compare gross pay with *total labour costing* on a regular basis. This involves reconciling:

- the *total wages and salaries expense* for a given period – ie what the employees are actually paid (before deductions) for the hours they have worked, and . . .

- the *total labour cost* allocated to the different departments on the basis of internal records of what time has been spent on what job (eg from clock cards, time sheets or job sheets) by means of coding numbers (normally input into the organisation's computer system)

It would seem logical that if the employees of a business have worked, say, a total of 10,000 hours in a week, then the *recorded* hours worked for the various departments would also be 10,000. Errors, however, do occur and it may be the case that the *recorded* hours (from timesheets, jobsheets etc) are fewer than the *actual* hours worked. The result of this is that one or more departments may be *undercharged* for the cost of the labour (the wages paid for the hours that have been worked in that department). This can happen in a number of ways:

- employees have forgotten to record on their timesheets the reference code for work done for a particular department

- *idle time* – eg time spent not working if a computer breaks down – employees will be paid for this time, but it may not be on the timesheets

Study the following diagram and the text that follows to see what happens when gross pay amounts to £2,000 more than total labour costing.

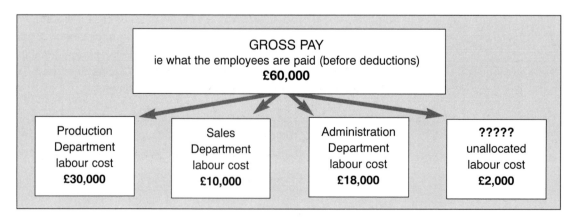

There is a difference of £2,000 which will have to be investigated. A costing clerk may well have to examine all the timesheets or jobcards and see if there are any codes missing or any idle time which is not allocated to a department. It may be, for example that a series of computer 'crashes' in the Administration Department resulted in the loss of £2,000 of 'time' which was not allocated to that department. Once this 'idle time' is identified, it will be charged to the Administration Department. Gross pay and total labour costing will be reconciled.

Gross pay £60,000   =   Total labour costing £60,000

The labour cost allocation will then be as follows:

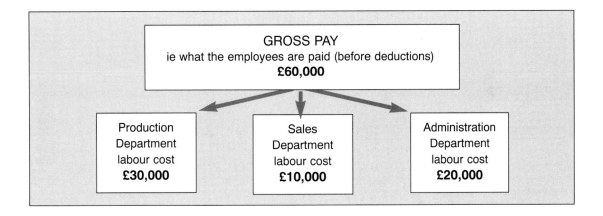

CHAPTER SUMMARY

- The first stage of payroll processing is the calculation and payment of wages and salaries.

- The final stage of payroll processing is the transfer of the payroll totals into the ledger accounts of the organisation.

- The ledgers will be maintained either in a paper-based system or (increasingly) on computer file.

- The totals that will be posted to the accounts include:
    - the gross pay of the employees
    - the net pay of the employees
    - income tax deductions
    - National Insurance contributions (employer's and employees')
    - pension contributions (employer's and employees')

- The amounts will normally be posted to

  - the appropriate ledger account and to

  - a Wages & Salaries Control Account

  The items that make up a Wages & Salaries Control Account are shown below.

Dr	Wages & Salaries Control Account				Cr	
Bank	Net pay	£££	**Wages & salaries**	Gross wages	£££
Inland Revenue	Income tax due	£££		Employer's NICs	£££
	National Insurance (employer's)	£££		Employer's pension contribution	£££
	National Insurance (employees')	£££			
Pension Fund	Employer's contribution	£££			
	Employees' contribution	£££			
Other deductions	eg, GAYE, SAYE	£££			
		£££			£££

Note: the items in bold type are the actual accounts which will be shown in the control account; the items in lighter type are the payroll totals which make up those account entries.

- The payroll process is useful in that it allows an organisation to analyse the *labour cost* of subdivisions of its operations such as departments and products.

- The labour costing process is made simpler by the *coding* of work carried out in departments, and on products and specific jobs.

- Another part of the payroll process is the reconciling of gross pay to the total labour costs of the organisation. Any discrepancies should be investigated and reported where appropriate.

KEY TERMS	**control account**	a 'master account' used for bringing together entries made on subsidiary accounts
	subsidiary accounts	accounts connected with a single function in the organisation (eg payroll); entries in all cases are made to both control and subsidiary accounts

coding

the giving of an unique code to labour carried out in specific cost areas of an organisation, eg in departments or on different products

total labour costing

the total estimated cost of labour for the different operations of an organisation

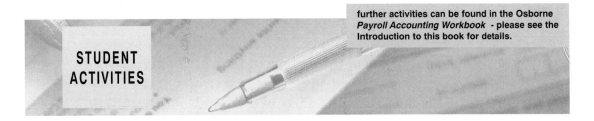

further activities can be found in the Osborne _Payroll Accounting Workbook_ - please see the Introduction to this book for details.

STUDENT ACTIVITIES

The following data will form the basis for multiple choice questions 9.1 to 9.3.

The payroll system of Home Fires Limited has recorded the following totals for the month of July:

gross pay	£350,780
income tax deducted by PAYE	£69,500
NIC (employees' contribution)	£31,450
NIC (employer's contribution)	£35,085
pension: paid by the employees by deduction from pay	£7,500
pension: employer's contribution	£7,500

9.1 The total payment to the Inland Revenue for the month will be

(a) £100,950

(b) £104,585

(c) £15,000

(d) £136,035

Choose one option from (a) to (d).

9.2 The total wages & salaries expense to the employer will be

(a) £350,780

(b) £462,865

(c) £393,365

(d) £308,195

Choose one option from (a) to (d).

9.3   The total net pay to employees will be

(a)   £242,330

(b)   £249,830

(c)   £389,730

(d)   £350,780

Choose one option from (a) to (d).

9.4   Pegasus Limited has recorded the following payroll totals for the month of October:

gross pay	£101,500
income tax deducted by PAYE	£20,500
NIC (employees' contribution)	£9,860
NIC (employer's contribution)	£10,150
pension: employer's contribution (non-contributory pension)	£7,500

(a)   Calculate the total payroll cost to the employer

(b)   Calculate the payment due to the Inland Revenue

(c)   Calculate the net pay due to employees

(d)   Draw up double entry accounts for Wages & Salaries, Inland Revenue, Pension Fund, Bank, and Wages & Salaries Control and post the relevant entries. Assume a nil opening balance for each account. You do not need to balance the accounts.

9.5   Jasons Wool Shop has recorded the following payroll totals for the month of October:

gross pay	£50,000
income tax deducted by PAYE	£11,110
NIC (employees' contribution)	£4,985
NIC (employer's contribution)	£5,010
pension: paid by the employees by deduction from pay	£1,100
pension: employer's contribution	£1,100

(a)   Calculate the total payroll cost to the employer

(b)   Calculate the payment due to the Inland Revenue

(c)   Calculate the amount due to the Pension Fund

(d)   Calculate the net pay due to employees

(e)   Draw up double entry accounts for Wages & Salaries, Inland Revenue, Pension Fund, Bank, and Wages & Salaries Control and post the relevant entries. Assume a nil opening balance for each account. You do not need to balance the accounts.

9.6   Rainbow Paints manufactures a wide range of domestic and industrial paints and coatings.

Gross pay for last year totalled £100,000.

Labour costs allocated to the departments for the same period, according to the company's internal records were:

Administration	£10,000
Production	£60,000
Sales	£10,000
Distribution	£15,000

The difference of £5,000 between total gross pay and total labour costing was placed to a suspense account.

Staff investigating the difference found that:

- Stan and Olly in the Production Department had missed off codes relating to £1,000 of labour cost

- Martin and Ahmed in Administration had £2,000 of idle time not allocated a code

- Derby and Joan in Sales had failed to record codes for £2,000 of labour cost

(a)   What was the total labour cost of each department?

(b)   Why was it important to clear the suspense account by finding the reasons for the difference?

10 SICK PAY AND MATERNITY PAY

this chapter covers . . .

In this chapter we look at the payment to employees of sick pay and maternity pay. Although many employers operate schemes whereby they automatically pay their employees when they are off sick or are away from work to have a baby, the Government has passed legislation to ensure that employees are paid a guaranteed minimum rate when they are absent from work for these reasons.

We will therefore examine the workings of

- Statutory Sick Pay

- Statutory Maternity Pay

As noted below, these two types of payment are not included in the NVQ Accounting Level 2 requirements. They have been included in this tutorial for use by students studying on other payroll courses and for practical guidance of the general reader.

NVQ PERFORMANCE CRITERIA COVERED

The subject matter of this chapter is not in the NVQ specifications, but has been included at the request of a number of teaching centres.

STATUTORY BENEFITS

An employer has a duty in law (a 'statutory' duty) to pay certain benefits to employees:

- *Statutory Sick Pay (SSP)* to most employees over the age of 16 who are away sick from work for four or more days (including weekends) in a row
- *Statutory Maternity Pay (SMP)* to female employees who are away from work to have a baby

Some of this money paid out by the employer can be reclaimed by deducting it from the National Insurance contributions (NICS) due each month:

- SSP – a certain amount is recoverable if SSP paid out exceeds a certain percentage of total NICS paid for the month
- SMP – between 92% and 100%, depending on the size of the business

STATUTORY SICK PAY (SSP)

Statutory Sick Pay (SSP) must by law be paid to most employees who are ill for four or more days in a row. This period of sickness, which includes non-working days such as weekends, is called a *Period of Incapacity for Work* (PIW).

SSP is paid for *qualifying days* (days that 'qualify' for SSP). A qualifying day is a day which an employee normally works, ie usually Monday to Friday. SSP is not normally paid for the first three qualifying days which are known as *waiting days*. In basic terms, an employee is *normally* paid SSP from the fourth working day of the illness.

In order to qualify for SSP the employee has to earn at least the amount at which National Insurance contributions become payable. Some employers may 'top up' or replace this payment to provide the employee with full pay for the period of sickness, but here the employer stands the cost of the 'top up' or replacement pay. The object of the scheme is for the State to ensure that sick employees receive an income while they are incapacitated, whether it be because of serious illness or a bad curry.

The Inland Revenue issues tables setting out the rate of SSP and SMP. For example, in the tax year 1999/2000 the weekly rate of SSP is £59.55. If the employee worked a five day week (5 qualifying days) he or she would receive a daily rate of £11.91 (ie the weekly rate of £59.55 divided by 5).

Employees who are *not* entitled to SSP include:

- people who earn less than the NIC Lower Earnings Limit (ie they do not pay National Insurance)
- people over 65

- employees contracted to work for less than three months
- people receiving Statutory Maternity Pay (SMP)
- people outside the European Economic Area

procedure when an employee reports sick

If, for example, an employee called Bob is off sick, he will normally notify the employer if he cannot get to work, then:

- if he is off sick for less than seven days he will on return to work fill in an Employee's Statement of Sickness (Form SC2), or the employer's internal form saying what was wrong with him
- if he is off sick for more than seven days he will need a doctor's note

questions for the employer to ask to determine SSP

How many days has the employee been sick?

- 1 to 3 days – no SSP is payable – the employer is responsible for any sick pay
- 4 days or more (which can include weekends) – this is a Period of Incapacity for Work (PIW), and SSP is probably payable

Has the employee had another Period of Incapacity for Work (PIW) within the last eight weeks?

If this is the case (the SSP Tables issued by the Inland Revenue will help here), then this will affect the number of days for which SSP is payable. In effect one PIW will link with an earlier one, and SSP will be payable for all of the qualifying days in the later PIW, including the first three qualifying days (see below).

For how many days is SSP payable?

SSP is payable for qualifying days. A qualifying day is a day on which an employee normally works, ie usually Monday to Friday. SSP is never payable for the first qualifying three days of a Period of Incapacity for Work (PIW), unless the PIW links with an earlier PIW (ie if the employee has received SSP within the previous eight weeks). In simple terms, normally if an employee is off sick, he is paid SSP from the fourth working day up to a maximum of 28 weeks.

What is the daily rate of SSP?

The daily rate of SSP is the weekly rate (£59.55 in the 1999/2000 tax year) divided by the number of qualifying days in that week.

CASE STUDY

BOB FALLS SICK

example one

Bob falls ill with the 'flu' on Monday morning and keeps to his bed until the next Sunday afternoon. He normally works Monday to Friday, ie the qualifying days are Monday to Friday. He has not been off sick in the previous six months. When will he receive SSP? After the three waiting days.

PIW						
MONDAY	TUESDAY	WEDNESDAY	THURSDAY	FRIDAY	SATURDAY	SUNDAY
waiting day	waiting day	waiting day	qualifying day	qualifying day	non-qualifying day	non-qualifying day
NO SSP	NO SSP	NO SSP	SSP PAID	SSP PAID	NO SSP	NO SSP

example two

Two weeks later Bob has a relapse, and is off sick for a further Monday to Friday. He now has two linking Periods of Incapacity for Work (PIWs), and so there are no waiting days in the second PIW.

PIW						
MONDAY	TUESDAY	WEDNESDAY	THURSDAY	FRIDAY	SATURDAY	SUNDAY
qualifying day	qualifying day	qualifying day	qualifying day	qualifying day	non-qualifying day	non-qualifying day
SSP PAID	SSP PAID	SSP PAID	SSP PAID	SSP PAID	NO SSP	NO SSP

problems with weekends and SSP

Confusion is sometimes caused by weekends (or non-working days) when calculating eligibility for SSP. Remember the following:

- a Period of Incapacity for Work (PIW) can include non-working days, eg the weekend
- but . . . calculations for SSP are based on qualifying days, ie working days
- and . . . the first three qualifying days (ie not normally Saturday or Sunday) are waiting days for which SSP is not payable

For example, if Bob in the Case Study falls ill on a Sunday, and there is no previous linking PIW, the PIW begins on Sunday, but the first of the three qualifying days is Monday, and he will receive SSP from Thursday, the first qualifying day, as in example one on the previous page.

recovering SSP – Percentage Threshold Scheme

If the employer qualifies under the Percentage Threshold Scheme (PTS), the employer can reclaim a certain amount of SSP. How does the employer qualify? If the employer in any one month pays out in SSP more than 13% of gross Class 1 National Insurance contributions then the employer can recover the excess. For example, suppose total gross monthly National Insurance contributions are £1,000 and the employer pays out £200 in SSP, an excess of £70 has been paid. (13% of £1,000 is £130, and £200 minus £130 is £70). This £70 can be reclaimed by deducting it from the monthly payment of NICS to the Inland Revenue.

STATUTORY MATERNITY PAY (SMP)

Statutory Maternity Pay (SMP) is paid to an employee who is away from work to have and look after a baby, even if she does not intend to return to work. It is payable for a period of up to 18 weeks. Like SSP it is payable by the employer and recoverable by deduction from National Insurance contributions paid by the employer to the Inland Revenue. Unlike most SSP, most or all of SMP is recoverable, plus an allowance for NIC paid on the SMP.

procedure when an employee becomes pregnant

If an employee reports that she is pregnant, an employer should

- ask for medical evidence of the due date of the baby (normally on Form MATB1 from the doctor)
- look at the SMP Tables issued by the Department of Social Security and find the Expected Week of Confinement (when the baby is due) in Column 1, then read off in Column 2 the qualifying week (15 weeks before the confinement week); this qualifying week is critical for the payment of SMP (see below)

does the employee qualify for SMP?

In order to qualify for SMP, a woman must

- be continuously employed for at least 26 weeks into the qualifying week (see above)
- be paid at least the NIC lower earnings limit (ie she must be paying NICs)

- still be pregnant in the 11th week before the due date, or have had the baby by then
- stop working for the employer when payment is to be made
- not be taken into legal custody!
- give 21 days' notice of the start of the Maternity Pay Period

how much SMP?

- higher rate – for the first six weeks of payment: 90% of the employee's average weekly earnings
- lower rate – payable for the remaining 12 weeks of the Maternity Pay Period at £59.55 per week (1999/2000 tax year)

what is the time schedule for payment of SMP?

The choice of the timing of the Maternity Pay Period (MPP), ie when SMP is paid, lies with the pregnant woman. She may, for instance want to carry on working as long as possible, and use the time off work and MPP for the period of sleepless nights after the birth. There are, however, certain constraints:

- the MPP cannot start before the eleventh week before the Expected Week of Confinement
- the latest MPP can start is the Sunday after the birth of the child

Look at the diagram set out below – time runs horizontally:

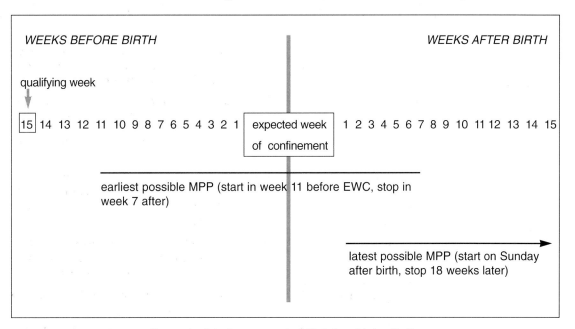

time schedule for payment of Statutory Maternity Pay

recovery of SMP by the employer

SMP is recorded on the employee's P11 deductions sheet, together with SMP recovered; NIC and income tax are deducted where appropriate. SMP is recovered when the monthly return of NIC and income tax is made to the Inland Revenue. Normally 92% is recoverable, but 'small' employers can claim back 100%. An additional percentage of gross SMP is also recoverable by small employers at the same time to compensate for administration.

employer's maternity pay schemes

It must be stressed that SMP is a state benefit and may be 'topped up' by an employer's maternity payment scheme which may be offered as part of the pay package offered with a job. SMP represents the minimum benefit payable, and must be paid where the woman qualifies for it.

CHAPTER SUMMARY

- Statutory Sick Pay (SSP) is paid by employers to most employees who are away sick from work for four or more days in a row.

- SSP is payable only for qualifying days in a Period of Incapacity for Work. The first three qualifying days of an unlinked PIW are waiting days for which SSP is not payable.

- Statutory Maternity Pay is paid by employers to women who are away from work to have a baby; it is normally payable for 18 weeks.

- Some SSP and most SMP is normally recoverable from the Inland Revenue; the claims are set against National Insurance contributions.

KEY TERMS

Statutory Sick Pay (SSP)	the minimum amount required by law to be paid to qualifying employees who are off work sick for four days or more
waiting day	a day on which no SSP is paid (normally the first three qualifying days of illness)
qualifying day	a day on which the employee normally works
Period of Incapacity for Work (PIW)	the period during which the employee is unable to work through illness (it includes non-working days, waiting days and qualifying days)
Statutory Maternity Pay (SMP)	the minimum amount required by law to be paid to qualifying employees who are off work to have or look after a baby
Expected Week of Confinement	the week in which the baby is due (abbreviated to EWC)
Maternity Pay Period (MPP)	the 18 week period during which SMP is payable

**STUDENT
ACTIVITIES**

background to activities

You work as payroll clerk at Osborne Biscuits, a food company which employs 350 people on weekly payroll, including production line workers, packers and other clerical staff. Your particular area of work is dealing with payment of SSP and SMP. Set out below are some of the transactions with which you will have to deal.

Note: the company works a Monday to Friday working week; Saturday and Sunday are not qualifying days for SSP; the daily SSP rate is therefore the weekly rate divided by five. The company does not operate its own sickness pay scheme nor a maternity pay scheme.

10.1 It is a Friday pay day in the current month. Calculate the Statutory Sick Pay due, where appropriate, for the employees listed below for the period Monday to Friday. Use current rates. State in each case:

- the waiting days, where applicable
- the qualifying days, where applicable, for which SSP is payable

(a) Bill Taylor, reported sick on Monday, still off sick on Friday; not off sick for the last six months; weekly pay £150.

(b) James Mason, reported sick on Monday, still off sick on Friday; not off sick for the last three months; weekly pay £250.

(c) Christine Thompson, reported sick on Monday still off sick on Friday; off sick for ten days (SSP paid) a month ago; weekly pay £150.

(d) Caroline Morgan, reported sick on Monday still off sick on Friday; off sick for ten days (SSP paid) a month ago; weekly pay £250.

(e) Bruno Hicks, reported sick on Wednesday, still off sick on Friday; never reported sick before; weekly pay £150.

(f) Luigi Brunello, reported sick on Tuesday, still off sick on Friday; not off sick for four months; weekly pay £150.

(g) Tom Talbot, reported sick on Tuesday, still off sick on Friday; off sick for ten days (SSP paid) a month ago; weekly pay £250.

(h) Trevor Davies, reported sick on Monday still off sick on Friday; off sick for ten days (SSP paid) a month ago; weekly pay £250. He claims that he started his illness last Saturday, and wants this to be taken into consideration.

(i) Vicky Mostyn, who is on maternity leave on SMP and two weeks away from the expected week of confinement, is rushed into hospital on Monday with high blood pressure; her husband Martin phones in to ask for sick pay.

(j) Andrea O'Shea, a student on a temporary one month contract, earning £50 a week, reported sick on Monday, still off sick on Friday. She has not been off sick before.

10.2 It is the third week of April. You receive the following enquiries about Statutory Maternity Pay. State how you would deal with them. Where appropriate calculate the rate of SMP that will be received. Use the SMP Tables produced by the Inland Revenue.

    (a)   Denise Jones is expecting a baby; her form MATB1 states that it is due in the third week in November. She has been working for Osborne Biscuits for 10 years, and her current average weekly pay is £200. She wants to know if she is eligible for SMP, when she can give up work, the period of time for which she will receive SMP, and how much she will receive.

    (b)   Angelica Rice is also expecting a baby; her form MATB1 states that it is due in the second week in December. She has been working for Osborne Biscuits for 12 months, and her current average weekly pay is £150. She wants to know if she is eligible for SMP, when she can give up work, the period of time for which she will receive SMP, and how much she will receive.

    (c)   Emma Stephenson is expecting a baby; her form MATB1 states that it is due in the last week in November. She has been working for Osborne Biscuits since March of the same year, and her current average weekly pay is £200. She wants to know if she is eligible for SMP, when she can give up work, the period of time for which she will receive SMP, and how much she will receive.

10.3 A new colleague joins the payroll team of Osborne Biscuits and asks:

    (a)   on what Inland Revenue forms will SSP and SMP be recorded?

    (b)   how much (if any) will the employer get back from the Inland Revenue?

    (c)   how is it reclaimed?

    (d)   how is it paid?

What would your answers be?

answers to student activities

CHAPTER 1: INTRODUCTION TO PAYROLL

1.1   See bullet points, page 3, paragraph 1.

1.2   True

1.3   False

1.4   (a) employed; (b) employed; (c) self-employed; (d) self-employed; (e) employed.

1.5   (a) the agency; (b) on invoice.

1.6   (a) see page 5; (b) see page 6.

1.7   False

1.8   The business; the Inland Revenue, HM Customs & Excise.

1.9   False (subject to any changes brought into effect by revisions to the Data Protection Act).

1.10   The need for accuracy; the prevention of fraud.

CHAPTER 2: CALCULATING GROSS PAY

2.1   (a) £1,000; (b) £2,500; (c) £1,500; (d) £650; (e) £465

2.2   (a) £125; (b) £180; (c) £220; (d) £130; (e) £150

2.3   (a) £210; (b) £240 + £18 = £258; (c) £240 + £72 = £312; (d) £240 + £90 = £330; (e) £234

2.4   Shift 1 £210 = £63 + £12 = £285;   Shift 2 £210 + £63 = £273;   Shift 3 £210 + £63 + £36 = £309

2.5   Week 1 £180; Week 2 £245; Week 3 £240.50; Week 4 £255

2.6

	Mead	Wallett	Tilley	Morioni	Total
	£	£	£	£	£
January	800	1,000	740	800	3,340
February	700	680	900	1,120	3,400
March	1,320	920	1,520	620	4,380

The Sales Manager will earn:

January	£1,667	(£1,500 + £167)
February	£1,670	(£1,500 + £170)
March	£1,719	(£1,500 + £219)

CHAPTER 3: PAY AS YOU EARN – INCOME TAX

3.1   (a)   Income tax; National Insurance contributions

     (b)   two from SAYE, GAYE, company pension contributions

3.2   (a)   Week 1, Month 1

     (b)   Week 5, Month 1

     (c)   Week 9, Month 3

     (d)   Week 12, Month 3

3.3   See page 27, paragraph 1.

3.4   (c)

3.5   Gross pay minus the tax allowance.

3.6   (b)

3.7   Removal of the last digit of the net tax allowance and adding of a letter, before or after the number.

3.8   P6

3.9   Consult your tax tables. The rates for 1999/2000 are: Starting Rate 10% (up to £1,500), Basic Rate 23% (£1,501 to £28,000), Higher Rate 40% over £28,000.

3.10

	Taxable Pay	Tax
A	£1,500	£1,500 @ 10% = £150
B	£9,500	£1,500 @ 10% = £150, plus £8,000 @ 23% = £1,840, total = £1,990
C	£22,500	£1,500 @ 10% = £150 plus £21,000 @ 23% = £4,830, total = £4,980
D	£35,500	£1,500 @ 10% = £150, plus £26,500 @ 23% = £6,095, plus £7,500 @ 40% = £3,000; total = £9,245

3.11   A 2.5%; B 14%; C 18%; D 23%

This shows clearly that the more you earn, the more proportionally is taken away in tax. Income tax therefore is a tax which helps to divert money from the wealthy to those who are less well-off.

3.12   (a)   Free Pay and Additional Pay for each tax week and month.

     (b)   Tax at Starting, Basic and Higher Rates of tax.

3.13   Employee payroll details (eg name, tax code, NI number).

PAYE deductions from gross pay (income tax and National Insurance contributions).

Note that it does not have columns for net pay or employer' NI contributions.

3.14

Employee	code	gross pay	free pay	taxable pay	tax	pay after tax
		£	£	£	£	£
R M Pitt	433L	250.00	83.45	166.55	34.42	215.58
N Doskopi	433L	275.00	83.45	191.55	40.17	234.83
N Trails	385H	450.00	74.22	375.78	82.49	367.51
N Emmer	375H	456.75	72.29	384.46	84.56	372.19
L Bowe	433L	195.00	83.45	111.55	21.77	173.23
M T Head	390H	305.00	75.18	229.82	48.91	256.09
Ray D Olligist	265H	380.00	51.14	328.86	71.68	308.32
N Jexion	433L	295.00	83.45	211.55	44.77	250.23

3.15   (a) £4,500 less £5,600 = minus £1,100; Code = K110

(b) £4,300 less £7,150 = minus £2,850; Code = K285

3.16   (a) BR; (b) DO

3.17   (a) B; (b) D

3.18   (a)   Basic personal allowance on a Week 1/Month 1 basis, used when no code has been issued.

(b)   Sam will be taxed at the starting and basic rates after allowing the basic code, but the free pay will be applied on a Week 1/Month 1 basis.

(c)   No. Sam should eventually get a refund when a tax code is issued by the tax office - the cumulative basis of the PAYE system should ensure that he pays the correct amount of tax.

CHAPTER 4: PAY AS YOU EARN – NATIONAL INSURANCE

4.1   False.

4.2   By PAYE – paid to the Inland Revenue.

4.3   (b)

4.4

	1a (£)	1b (£)	1c (£)	1d(£)	1e(£)
Week 1	66	17	47	12.24	6.45
Week 2	66	17	47	12.24	6.45
Week 3	66	17	64	16.02	8.15
Week 4	66	17	70	17.35	8.75
Week 5	66	17	72	17.79	8.95
Week 6	66	17	75	18.46	9.25

4.5   Employer's NI contribution quoted first, employee's second.

(a) nil/nil   (b) nil/£1.40   (c) £2.07/£3.40   (d) £22.81/£20.40

(e) £35.75/£31.00   (f) £14.27/£13.40   (g) £63.07/£43.40   (h) £93.57/£43.40

CHAPTER 5: FURTHER ASPECTS OF PAY AS YOU EARN – NATIONAL INSURANCE

5.1   False. A retired person will not be entitled if NICs have not been paid. Also a person may retire before the age at which entitlement starts (60 for women, 65 for men).

5.2   (a)

5.3   (a)   a pension based on the level of the final salary

(b)   a money purchase pension scheme

5.4   (a)   a company scheme, paid through the payroll

(b)   a independently provided scheme – arranged by the employee and paid direct (not through the employer)

5.5   Portability, tax relief on contributions.

5.6   (a)   payments are deducted before tax is calculated

(b)   payments are deducted after tax is calculated

(c)   none at all (not paid through payroll)

(d)   none (this only relates to National Insurance rates)

5.7   (a) £1,000 (£998 in Table)   (b) £950

5.8   Jim £750; Bob £875; and for Asif, Hans, Mel and Yousef £2,000 (£1,000 from 1 January 1999).

5.9   False. SSP can only be recovered if the amount paid out exceeds a certain percentage of NICs.

5.10   18 weeks. For the first six weeks at 90% of the employee's average weekly earnings, thereafter at £59.55 per week for 12 weeks (99/00 tax year).

CHAPTER 6: LEAVING AND STARTING EMPLOYMENT

6.1 (a) resignation, retirement, redundancy, dismissal, death

(b) Part 1 sent to the tax office by the issuer, Part 1a kept by the employee, Part 2 to the new employer, Part 3 sent by the new employer to the tax office

6.2 (a) new employee, with no P45, working for more than one week

(b) sent to the tax office (top and carbon copies)

6.3 (a) nothing – it has to be sorted between Anita and the tax office

(b) the amount should be entered on the P11 – tax code BR (no pay adjustment)

(c) a P45 has to be issued on the death of an employee – the letter 'D' will be recorded on the form which must be sent to the tax office

(d) give him back the Part 1a – it is his copy

(e) enter 'P' on P45 (box 10); the pay will be entered on the P11 for the new tax year

6.4 (a) the correct amount should be entered in box 12 of the P45; the P11 should be started off with the correct amount

(b) the part-time earnings will have to be entered on the P11 – he will be taxed on the Emergency Code (Week 1/Month 1) and a P46 will be forwarded to the tax office (with Statement B signed)

(c) a P11 will be completed with 'NI' in the tax code box – earnings and NICs will be entered in the appropriate columns

(d) a P46 will be sent to the tax office – Statement A will be signed and the details completed at the bottom of the form – a P11 will be started with the Emergency Code on a cumulative basis

CHAPTER 7: PAYING EMPLOYEES

7.1 (a) £300; (b) no; (c) Payroll number, NI Number, method of payment, tax code; (d) 5%

7.2 The other records are not complete – for example there is no employer's NI on the P11 or payslip.

7.3 Figures for the payroll sheet:

employee	total gross pay (£)	total deductions (£)	net pay (£)
A Lucas	133.75	23.97	109.78
D Hunt	120.00	23.99	96.01
I Atkins	133.75	23.72	110.03
C Robbins	126.88	19.85	107.03

Bottom line totals: basic £440.00 + overtime £34.38 + bonus £40.00 = £514.38

Income tax £52.50 + NIC £34.23 + savings £4.80 = £91.53; NIC (employer) £46.24; total £422.85

name	£20	£10	£5	£2	£1	50p	20p	10p	5p	2p	1p	total (£ p)
A Lucas	5	-	1	2	-	1	1	-	1	1	1	109.78
D Hunt	4	1	1		1	-	-	-	-	-	1	96.01
I Atkins	5	1	-	-	-	-	-	-	-	1	1	110.03
C Robbins	5	-	1	1	-	-	-	-	-	1	1	107.03
TOTAL	380.00	20.00	15.00	6.00	1.00	0.50	0.20	0.00	0.05	0.06	0.04	422.85

7.5   Security risk, expensive (labour intensive), wages have to be collected in person

7.6   The wages can be collected by a third party, but only with the written authority of the sick employee.

7.7   Security risk (the cheques have to be kept under lock and key); the time taken to process and check the cheques; the need for authorisation and signature/stamping.

7.8   The cheque is perfectly valid as long as the employer has an agreement with the bank for using the rubber stamp.

7.9   The credits and cheque will have to be taken to the bank for processing on Wednesday. The instructions should cover: completing the credits, checking the credits, drawing up a schedule listing the credits, totalling and checking the listing, preparing the cheque, obtaining authorisation and signature, taking the paperwork to the bank by the close of business on Wednesday.

7.10 (a)   BACS – supply of data direct to BACS by employer

   (b)   automated credit system through the employer's bank (routed via BACS)

   (c)   cash

CHAPTER 8: SENDING PAYMENTS AND RETURNS

8.1   False – small employers can pay quarterly.

8.2   (c)

8.3   See the key terms section at the back of the chapter.

8.4   (a)   P45 or top of the P11

   (b)   This is not included on the P14. The figures will be shown on the P14 submitted by the previous employer.

8.5   (a)   NIC (employer and employee) £763.52, Income tax £691.89, Total £1,455.41.

    (b)   Ditto.

8.6   (a)   All of the figures: pay, NICs (employee's, employee's + employer's) and income tax.

    (b)   NICs (employee's + employer's), income tax – for each employee.

    (c)   The differences are: NICs: £9,162.24 minus £8,993.56 = £168.68

                                Income tax £8,302.68 minus £8,144.88 = £157.80

As these differences are the same as the PAYE deduction figures for Matt Ease (month 12), it would seem likely that through some error, Matt Ease's PAYE has not been recorded on the P32 and has not been paid. The correct deductions will be recorded on the P14 summary on the P35 and the discrepancies will then show up at the bottom of the P35 form. The matter should be referred to supervisory level as a payment will have to be made to the Inland Revenue on a P30B payslip and a covering cheque for £326.48 raised. The supervisor will no doubt want to know how this error occurred and will take measures to ensure that it does not happen again!

CHAPTER 9: PAYROLL AND THE ACCOUNTING SYSTEM

9.1   (d)

9.2   (c)

9.3   (a)

9.4   (a)   £119,150

    (b)   £40,510

    (c)   £71,140

    (d)

account	debit (£)		credit (£)	
Wages & Salaries	Wages & Salaries Control	119,150		
Bank			Wages & Salaries Control	71,140
Inland Revenue			Wages & Salaries Control	40,510
Pension Fund			Wages & Salaries Control	7,500
Wages & Salaries Control	Bank	71,140	Wages & Salaries	119,150
	Inland Revenue	40,510		
	Pension Fund	7,500		

9.5 (a) £56,110

  (b) £21,105

  (c) £2,200

  (d) £32,805

account	debit (£)		credit (£)	
Wages & Salaries	Wages & Salaries Control	56,110		
Bank			Wages & Salaries Control	32,805
Inland Revenue			Wages & Salaries Control	21,105
Pension Fund			Wages & Salaries Control	2,200
Wages & Salaries Control	Bank	32,805	Wages & Salaries	56,110
	Inland Revenue	21,105		
	Pension Fund	2,200		

9.6 (a)

Administration	£12,000
Production	£61,000
Sales	£12,000
Distribution	£15,000
TOTAL	£100,000

  (b) If the causes of the difference had not been identified, the annual cost of running the relevant departments would be incorrectly calculated. The departments would appear to be more efficient than they actually were.

CHAPTER 10: SICK PAY AND MATERNITY PAY

10.1 (a) Bill Taylor, no linking; waiting days Monday, Tuesday, Wednesday; Qualifying days (QD) Thursday and Friday, paid 2/5 weekly rate.

  (b) James Mason, no linking; waiting days Monday, Tuesday, Wednesday; Qualifying days (QD) Thursday and Friday, paid 2/5 weekly rate.

  (c) C Thompson, PIW links, QD Monday to Friday, paid full weekly rate.

  (d) C Morgan, PIW links, QD Monday to Friday, paid full weekly rate.

  (e) B Hicks, none payable as Wednesday to Friday are waiting days.

  (f) L Brunello, no linking PIW, waiting days Tuesday to Thursday; QD Friday, paid 1/5 weekly rate.

  (g) T Talbot, PIW links, QD Tuesday to Friday, paid 4/5 weekly rate.

  (h) T Davies, PIW links, QD Monday to Friday, paid full weekly rate.

  (i) V Mostyn, no pay (on SMP).

  (j) A O'Shea, no pay, earning less than threshold.

10.2 The dates and rates, which change from year-to-year, should be obtained from the latest tables published by the Inland Revenue.

(a) Denise Jones: qualifying week will be in early August and the earliest date for payment early September. Amount 90% x 6 x £200 = £1,080 plus current rate x 12.

(b) Angelica Rice: qualifying week late August, earliest date for payment late September. Pay 90% x £150 x 6 = £810 plus current rate x 12.

(c) Emma Stephenson: no SMP as she has started work too late to qualify.

10.3 (a) Forms P11, P32, P35, P14/P60.

(b) SSP only if PTS scheme operates.

SMP 92%, or 100% if the employer qualifies for Small Employer's Relief.

(c) By deduction from gross NIC due monthly.

(d) Via payroll as gross pay.

INDEX